THE MARK OF THE BEAST

FROM CREATION TO REVELATION

ROBYN AND BRANDI CUNNINGHAM

The Mark of the Beast: From Creation to Revelation
Copyright 2024 by Robyn and Brandi Cunningham
Published by Robyn and Brandi Cunningham

All rights reserved. No part of this book may be reproduced, stored in a retrieval system, or transmitted in any form or by any means—electronic, mechanical, photocopy, recording, or otherwise—without prior written permission of the copyright owner. Please send permission requests to firesidegrace@yahoo.com

All Scripture quotations, unless otherwise indicated, are from the King James Version and are in the public domain.

Scriptures marked (NKJV) are taken from the NEW KING JAMES VERSION (NKJV): Scripture taken from the NEW KING JAMES VERSION®. Copyright© 1982 by Thomas Nelson, Inc. Used by permission. All rights reserved.

Scripture quotations marked (NIV) taken from The Holy Bible, New International Version® NIV®
Copyright © 1973, 1978, 1984, 2011 by Biblica, Inc. Used with permission. All rights reserved worldwide.

Scripture quotations marked (TPT) are from The Passion Translation®. Copyright © 2017, 2018, 2020 by Passion & Fire Ministries, Inc. Used by permission. All rights reserved. ThePassionTranslation.com.

Scripture quotations marked (CSB) are from the The Christian Standard Bible. Copyright © 2017 by Holman Bible Publishers. Used by permission. Christian Standard Bible®, and CSB® are federally registered trademarks of Holman Bible Publishers, all rights reserved.

Scripture quotations marked (NLT) are from the Holy Bible, New Living Translation, copyright © 1996, 2004, 2015 by Tyndale House Foundation. Used by permission of Tyndale House Publishers, Inc., Carol Stream, Illinois 60188. All rights reserved.

Scripture quotations marked (ESV) are from The Holy Bible, English Standard Version. ESV® Text Edition: 2016. Copyright © 2001 by Crossway Bibles, a publishing ministry of Good News Publishers.

Scriptures marked (AMP) taken from the Amplified Version, Copyright © 2015 The Lockman Foundation, La Habra, CA 90631. All rights reserved.

Scriptures marked (NASB 1995) taken from the New American Standard Bible®, Copyright © 1960, 1971, 1977, 1995 by The Lockman Foundation. All rights reserved.

Scripture quotations marked (ABPE) are taken from the ARAMAIC BIBLE IN PLAIN ENGLISH, 2010 Copyright©, Rev. David Bauscher, Lulu Enterprises Incorporated, 2010

Scriptures marked (BLB) taken from The Holy Bible, Berean Literal Bible, BLB Copyright ©2016, 2018 by Bible Hub Used by Permission. All Rights Reserved Worldwide.

Scriptures marked (BSB) The Holy Bible, Berean Standard Bible, BSB Copyright ©2016, 2018 by Bible Hub
Used by Permission. All Rights Reserved Worldwide.

All emphasis in Scripture is the author's own.

ISBNs: 978-1-953143-07-5 (Paperback)
978-1-953143-08-2 (Ebook)

Printed in the U.S.A.

I would like to dedicate this book to my wife, Brandi. Thank you for listening to me teach about the origin of demons, dinosaurs, and aliens for the last five years. Your encouragement is why I could press in despite the spiritual warfare that came because of writing this book.

Contents

Disclaimer	7
Introduction	9
Chapter 1: Debunking The Pre-Adamic Race	13
Chapter 2: Who Are the Bene Ha-Elohim?	23
Chapter 3: The Flesh of Angels and Men	33
Chapter 4: The Corruption of All Flesh	47
Chapter 5: The Origin of Dinosaurs	57
Chapter 6: Nimrod's Technology	63
Chapter 7: The Division of the Continents	75
Chapter 8: The Biblical Origin of Demons	81
Chapter 9: How Are Dead Spirits Still on the Earth?	97
Chapter 10: The Substance of Nightmares	107
Chapter 11: Unraveling the Mystery of the Beast	119
Chapter 12: Daniel's Visions	123
Chapter 13: Daniel's Dream	129
Chapter 14: The Four Beast Kingdoms	133
Chapter 15: The Four Kingdoms Become One	139
Chapter 16: Discerning the Times	145
Chapter 17: The Time and Weapons of His Indignation	153
Chapter 18: Leviathan in the Last Days	161
Chapter 19: Leviathan and Typhon	169
Chapter 20: The Great Deception	177
Chapter 21: How to Prepare	183

Disclaimer

Within the pages of this book are end-time mysteries that may be new and shocking to you. Some of what you are about to read may terrify you, but do not be dismayed. This book is meant to be a biblical study guide to equip the body of Christ for the end of days, and dispel some common misconceptions about the Antichrist, Satan, and the mark of the beast.

I believe the Bible is inerrant in its original language. It is very common for a translation from one language to another to inadequately convey the message, idea, or meaning of some words or phrases. This is fairly common with Old Testament Hebrew being translated into English. Examples of this are highlighted in this book. That does not mean that we can't trust the Bible. It simply means that we need to always be studying the Word so we may know the appropriate context and translation of the original text in order to better understand the message the authors were trying to present.

You will also find that with Hebrew words, the spelling often changes when different uses of a word are employed. These subtle changes are not inaccuracies; they are variations of the root word.

While reading this book, you will assuredly come across things you haven't heard before and those that may challenge your current understanding of the end of days. I beseech you to please challenge this message with the Word of God, pray over it, and ask the Lord for revelation and understanding of what you are reading.

The Mark of the Beast

If you have objections, challenges, or questions, please feel free to contact us through our website at www.FiresideGrace.com.

I pray this scripture will bless your soul and give you hope in any time or situation that you feel discouraged, hopeless, or despondent.

> Our soul waits for the LORD; He *is* our help and our shield. For our heart shall rejoice in Him, Because we have trusted in His holy name. Let Your mercy, O LORD, be upon us, Just as we hope in You. (Psalm 33:20-22, NKJV)

Introduction

I had been under the impression, before I was ever a Christian, that fallen angels were demons. This is the accepted and acceptable belief of the church by and large. I never questioned that narrative until one day a friend of mine, who has since turned their back on Christianity, asked me, "If Scripture tells us that the angels that fell are chained in hell, then what are demons, and why are they responsible for making people sin and carry out the devil's will?" I didn't have an answer for that. Little did I know, that conversation would be the catalyst that propelled me into discovering the hidden-in-plain-sight mystery of the origin of demons.

In today's church culture, it is largely believed that demons are responsible for a variety of issues that plague mankind. We typically call these issues "sins" or "works of the flesh." Paul teaches us the fruit of the flesh (works of the flesh):

> Now the works of the flesh are evident, which are: adultery, fornication, uncleanness, lewdness, idolatry, sorcery, hatred, contentions, jealousies, outbursts of wrath, selfish ambitions, dissensions, heresies, envy, murders, drunkenness, revelries, and the like; of which I tell you beforehand, just as I also told you in time past, that those who practice such things will not inherit the kingdom of God. (Galatians 5:19-21, NKJV)

The Mark of the Beast

Do you see the similarities between the work of the flesh and the work of demons? Take note of this; it will be critical for understanding the revelation contained in this book.

Have you ever wondered why demons are responsible for luring people to do things that stimulate the flesh and produce such works of the flesh? Let me explain a few things about the origin of demons and the purposes for why they do what they do.

The belief in the church today is that the fallen angels are demons. That's interesting because the Hebrews of the Old Testament, Jesus, God, and the Christians of the New Testament always differentiate between angels and demons.

> For if God did not spare angels when they sinned, but sent them to hell, putting them in chains of darkness to be held for judgment. (2 Peter 2:4, NKJV)

> And the angels who did not keep their positions of authority but abandoned their proper dwelling—these he has kept in darkness, bound with everlasting chains for judgment on the great Day. (Jude 6)

If demons are fallen angels, and they are bound in chains until the day of judgment, how can they actively possess people and otherwise operate freely, yet be held in chains in hell?

The answer is: they are not. Demons are not fallen angels, and they are not the disembodied spirits of a pre-adamic race. I will now present to you evidence to support what I am telling you. You are probably thinking I am a heretic or a blasphemer, or preaching a false doctrine, but if you would, please allow me to show you why I believe demons are not fallen angels.

Before we progress any further, I want to emphasize that there is a level of warfare that comes with the topics discussed in this book. While authoring it, I would often see spirits coming in and trying to hinder the writing of this book. I would like to take this time to say a prayer that will hopefully help to combat these spirits.

Introduction

Lord, I ask You to place a hedge of protection around all those that read this book. May their ears, eyes, and mind be open to hear You through any murkiness or confusion the Enemy tries to place on them. May all strongholds be broken here and now, and all thoughts brought into submission and obedience to You. Please protect and bless all who read this book, and please draw those who are endarkened into true enlightenment through Jesus Christ, the Light of the World. In Jesus's name I pray. Amen.

Chapter 1: Debunking The Pre-Adamic Race

When I first became a Christian, I didn't even understand what I had just done! I didn't know what "Christian" meant. I wasn't discipled. I didn't live in a Christian home. I didn't go to church. For some odd reason though, I wanted to be a pastor, and I wanted to teach.

I had simply been led in a prayer of salvation at a bus stop in Utica, New York. I have no idea who the man was that prayed for me; no idea what to do next; no Bible; no inkling of what Christianity even was really, except a bunch of dos and don'ts. When I got home that day, my grandma asked me, "What did you do today, Robbie?" I replied, "I guess I accepted Jesus today, whatever that means."

Today, I am a teacher to the body of Christ. Several years ago, I had an encounter with Jesus in which He informed me of my calling; in a nutshell, I am called to be a teacher to the body of Christ. Jesus said to me, "You have been called to raise up the prophetic generation that was birthed shortly before Kim Clement came home, and to teach people to hear the voice of God through dream interpretation."

The really crazy thing is that I had no clue who Kim Clement was. I was just introduced to him in 2018 by my wife, and I hadn't thought of him at all after that until years later when I had this encounter. I still, to this day, have only heard probably two or three of his teachings and

The Mark of the Beast

maybe two of the songs he wrote. However, I find it interesting that when I got saved, I learned how to hear God's voice through John Paul Jackson's teachings as I was pursuing dream interpretation. I learned that God speaks in several ways, and as I began to dig into the Word of God so I could accurately interpret dreams, I learned how to interpret what God is saying at any given time. I learned that God speaks the same way in the Bible as He speaks in dreams, as He speaks in real life—and I learned how to decipher His messages.

I believe that God is speaking all the time, but we aren't listening. I also learned how to read the white of the Bible—or read between the lines as some would say. That has helped me to be able to get a clearer understanding of what is being said in the Bible.

Make no mistake though, I am not saying that I am infallible. However, I do believe that the Word of God in its original language is inerrant, and it does not contradict itself. That is the basis of how I study the Bible and how I discovered the things I reveal in this book.

This chapter is about a topic that I believe needs to be addressed. I feel it's only fair to consider this theory since I have received so many questions about it in the past. I never just make up my mind about a theological doctrine without investigating both sides and much prayer. That being said, let's dive into this.

The premise of the pre-adamic race states that there was a race of beings that existed on the earth before God created mankind. It says that the earth is much older than 6,000 years, and that Satan's angels are chained here on earth until the final judgment, due to some massive cataclysmic event that eradicated all of life on the earth.

Only God knows how long Adam and Eve were on the earth in its unfallen state. Though God made day and night, there would be no sun, moon, or stars for the telling of times and seasons until the fourth day. This tells us that the earth is older than the sun and the moon. That throws out the whole theory that the moon was a part of earth at some point and then separated. The idea that time started when God began creating doesn't really fit the bill because the sun, moon, and stars are what we use to keep track of time.

Chapter 1: Debunking The Pre-Adamic Race

I'd also like to point out that many believe the earth is much older than 6,000 years old. I do believe that it could and did exist for more than 6,000 years, but we wouldn't know that because there was no decay or destruction until after the fall of man. Scientists believe they can trace back the amount of time it took the universe to be created by using half-lives of certain elements, but that can't be the case because there was no decay or lifespan of anything until after the fall. We would have no way to tell how old something was before the fall of man for that reason.

Another premise of this theory begins with Genesis 1:1-2. Most people who believe in the pre-adamic race theory believe that these scriptures are mistranslated, and therefore, from where all the confusion is derived. Specifically, verse 2 is where the mistranslation comes into play.

> And the earth was without form, and void; and darkness was upon the face of the deep. And the Spirit of God moved upon the face of the waters. (Genesis 1:2)

The word that is claimed to be mistranslated is *chayatah*. This word means to become, calamity, ruin, to exist, and "I am." The idea that is portrayed behind the pre-adamic race theory is that this means the earth became formless and void. Since it became formless, it is believed that it was not formless at some point. However, this is the same word that is used when God says, "I AM THAT I AM," in Exodus 3:14. If this word implies that the earth became formless because of a calamity, then this implies that God isn't uncreated but came into being. The Word of God tells us that the LORD is uncreated, inhabits eternity, is immortal, is the Alpha and Omega, etc.

The next two words that are contested in the pre-adamic theory are *tohu* and *wabohu*. *Tohu*, according to Strong's Concordance, means formless, meaningless, or desolate. This word can also be translated as confusion, waste, empty, vain, and without form.[1]

---

1. "H8414 - tôû - Strong's Hebrew Lexicon (kjv)." Blue Letter Bible. Accessed 27 Feb, 2024. https://www.blueletterbible.org/lexicon/h8414/kjv/wlc/0-1.

The Mark of the Beast

The word *wabohu* means empty, void, or vacuous. According to Webster,[2] vacuous expands past just empty and void to being *vacant*, a closely related word which can mean to be empty of thought, or thoughtlessness. The pre-adamic theory uses this word in correlation to Isaiah 45:18 where the word *tohu* is used.

> For thus saith the LORD that created the heavens; God himself that formed the earth and made it; he hath established it, he created it not in vain, he formed it to be inhabited: I am the LORD; and there is none else.

According to the pre-adamic theory, Genesis 1:2 means the earth became chaotic, empty, a desolate wasteland, etc. And then God reformed the world and gave us the accounting of the new world where Adam was created. Isaiah 45:18 is then translated to indicate that God didn't create the world to be void, and that somehow His creation became void and without purpose. My problem with this idea is that it makes the Word of God contradict itself.

I was confused by what seemed to be a glaring contradiction in Genesis 1:2 and Isaiah 45:18. What I discovered was that it says He fashioned (*yatsab*) the earth so it wouldn't be formless or void. This means He didn't create it so it wouldn't have any meaning or purpose. If He had to fashion it, then this implies that it wasn't formed at first but was without shape and purpose. Therefore, He shaped it and gave it purpose.

To be created void (*tohu*) would indicate that something was created without a purpose. This lack of purpose is correlated to being a waste, pointless, or confused. I find this correlation of purposelessness and confusion to be an interesting revelation.

Confusion is one of the largest issues that Americans face today. Identity confusion, gender confusion, sexuality confusion, and other topics are prevalent in the media. We see it almost everywhere we go. You can rarely walk into a store and not be bombarded with evidence of

---

2. Webster's Collegiate Dictionary, s.v. "vacuous" and "vacant," (Sparingfield, Mass: G.C. Merriam Co., 1913). 897.

Chapter 1: Debunking The Pre-Adamic Race

some type of confusion. These people are in direct defiance of the Word of God. When a person doesn't line up with the Word of God, they will not accomplish the fullness of their purpose on this earth. If God created man from earth, and the earth was made to have a purpose, then mankind is made to have a purpose.

God did not create the earth to exist without purpose, nor did He create it to exist in emptiness and chaos. He spoke a word and began to form and shape this new reality that He created. It was created with a purpose and fashioned and formed to give shape to that purpose. It wasn't simply created fully formed and fashioned, or else He wouldn't have had to fashion the seas, the land, the beasts, the trees, man, and everything else.

The last idea that I would like to discuss is at what point Satan and the angels fell. According to the pre-adamic theory, Satan fell before the creation of man. However, I do not believe that is the case.

This is my hypothesis: Satan and the angels fell before Adam and Eve were cast out of the garden but not before Adam and Eve were created. The Word says that Satan was perfect in all his ways and that he walked among the fiery stones.

> Thou art the anointed cherub that covereth; and I have set thee so: thou wast upon the holy mountain of God; thou hast walked up and down amid the stones of fire. Thou wast perfect in thy ways from the day that thou wast created, till iniquity was found in thee. By the multitude of thy merchandise, they have filled the midst of thee with violence, and thou hast sinned: therefore, I will cast thee as profane out of the mountain of God: and I will destroy thee, O covering cherub, from the midst of the stones of fire. Thine heart was lifted up because of thy beauty, thou hast corrupted thy wisdom by reason of thy brightness: I will cast thee to the ground, I will lay thee before kings, that they may behold thee. Thou hast defiled thy sanctuaries by the multitude of thine iniquities, by the iniquity of thy traffic; therefore, will I bring

forth a fire from the midst of thee, it shall devour thee, and I will bring thee to ashes upon the earth in the sight of all of them that behold thee. (Ezekiel 28:14-18)

If we look at verse 18, we see that it says Satan defiled his sanctuaries. The word for defiled here is the same word that is translated "I cast you out as a profane thing." That word is *chalal*. It means to wound, to break one's promise, to defile, pollute, stain. There's isn't a time, except in this verse, where it is ever used to mean to cast down as profane. In this context, it is pointing out that something was done to the sanctuary for all to see. That action made the sanctuaries defiled. A sanctuary is a sacred place—a holy place—such as a temple or church.

I believe the part in verse 18 that says, "Thou hast defiled your sanctuaries by the iniquity of thy traffic," is referring to the time frame referenced in Jude 6, when the angels left their abodes in heaven.

Another indicator that leads me to believe this is referring to when the angels fell is that it uses the word "traffic" multiple times in this part of Scripture. The Hebrew word used here is *rekullah*. This word is derived from the root word *rakal*, which means to go about or wander about. This indicates that the type of trafficking or merchandising discussed here is not monetary gain as much as it appears to be referring to leaving their habitation and going somewhere they should not be and sharing information.

Satan was limited in some areas, but he was very knowledgeable in other areas. Satan was exchanging his knowledge elsewhere. How else would an angel who knows God face-to-face get other angels that knew God the same way as well? However, we see in 1 Peter 1:12 that angels don't know everything.

> To whom it was revealed that they were serving not themselves, but you, in those things which now have been proclaimed to you by those having proclaimed the gospel to you by *the* Holy Spirit having been sent from heaven, into which angels desire to look. (BLB)

Chapter 1: Debunking The Pre-Adamic Race

If you read that scripture in context, it is speaking of how prophets desired to know about Jesus. They wanted to know when He would come, etc. Peter said the Holy Spirit revealed those things to them. Then he said that those are things that angels desire to look upon. That indicates to me that angels can't understand the gospel message.

I find that to be laughable. Not that I am laughing at angels, but that Satan, who is a fallen angel, cannot understand the gospel. That is why Satan had Jesus crucified. He is limited, so the gospel makes no sense to him.

Also, Satan doesn't have three of the gemstones that are on the breastplate of judgment. Those three are: jacinth (Gad, who was a military strength and he who overcomes), agate (Asher, known for good food, happiness, and blessing), and amethyst (Issachar, scholars who understood dates and times). These three tribes and their blessings—or their jewels—indicated the gifting they walked in.

However, Satan didn't have those giftings. He is unable to overcome God, Jesus, or the Holy Spirit. He is unhappy, angry, not blessed but cursed, and has no good spiritual food to offer anyone. And he cannot predict the times and seasons. Satan has no idea when things will happen because it is not in his nature.

However, he must have had something that other angels did not. If that wasn't the case, then I can't fathom how he could have leveraged anything to gain the trust of angels. The evidence suggests that the fallen angels began to teach people about astrology and the stars. Satan didn't have that anointing because it was an Issachar anointing. Yet the evidence from past civilizations indicates that human beings across the globe suddenly had a vast knowledge of the stars.

Satan began to wander away from his habitation, and in doing so, he began to become corrupt. I believe this is when the sinful thoughts, pride, arrogance, and treachery occurred that are spoken of in Isaiah 14:12-14:

> How art thou fallen from heaven, O Lucifer, son of the morning! how art thou cut down to the ground, which didst weaken the nations, or thou hast said in thine heart,

The Mark of the Beast

I will ascend into heaven, I will exalt my throne above the stars of God: I will sit also upon the mount of the congregation, in the sides of the north: I will ascend above the heights of the clouds; I will be like the most High.

We see in verse 12 that Satan is the *Naphalta* (second person masculine singular) or fallen from heaven. He was the first angel to fall. When multiple angels fell, they became Nephilim. In Genesis 6:4, the word "Nephilim" is a masculine, plural noun. So, we see that the Nephilim were all referenced or regarded as male. This may sound puzzling, but God also referred to Adam and Eve both as "Adam" despite one being female and one being male. In Genesis 5:2, it says in Hebrew that God called them both man and ha-adam. If you look back at the book of Genesis, it was Adam who called Eve "Eve," and it was Adam who called Eve "woman." You can still tell who was male and female on earth, but in heaven, you are beyond that in ways that we can't perceive now.

In verse 14, we see that Satan didn't say he would be like God. It says he will ascend to the dark clouds, *adamah elohim*. What it says in Hebrew is, "I will ascend to the high place, thicket, or dark cloud, *adamah elohim*. The word *adamah* is the way it is spelled. Strong's assumes that it is a derivative of the word *demah*, but the actual spelling in this verse is *aleph, dalet, mem, hey*. The word *adamah* (Strong's 127) is spelled the exact same way.

The word *adamah* means country, earth, soil, ground, husband, land, and is derived directly from the word *adam*. The word *adam* means ruddy, or red, and refers to the color of clay that was used to create Adam in the book of Genesis.

This implies, or even straightforward tells us, that Satan didn't want to be God—he wanted to be man, who was called *elohim*. This is not the only time we see that man is called *elohim* in Scripture. Jesus calls us *elohim* in John 10:34, referring to Psalm 82:6, in which mankind is referred to as the sons of God, or bene ha-Elohim.

Here's something to think about: Why would Satan say that he was going to ascend to the mountain of God if he hadn't fallen already? He wouldn't have to go up to the place that God was in if he was still a

Chapter 1: Debunking The Pre-Adamic Race

covering cherub that walked among the fiery stones. That means that he covered God with his wings, just like the cherubim that are still at the throne. He had the highest position as an angel. However, here he is saying, "I will be like *adamah* and go up there."

It's a peculiar thing to think that Satan fell before Adam and Eve did. That means that Satan, being evil, wasn't catching them off guard because he had already fallen. They were higher than him. Do you see how subtle Satan is? He had to begin to corrupt creation, get angels, get a dragon to do his bidding, etc. Otherwise, Adam and Eve would have known that Satan was trying to mislead them. That's my conjecture anyway.

Chapter 2: Who Are the Bene Ha-Elohim?

Lucifer looked upon God and gazed intently at His beauty and majesty. He approached the throne and walked in the most holy of holy places: the platform where the throne of God rests. He walked amidst a white, fiery hot, oceanic blue sapphire stone platform amongst his brothers. As his jewels and instruments adorned him, he shone like the sun itself. The only beauty that was greater than his own was the splendor of Elohim, the Lord God Jehovah. Lucifer spread his wings in a display of radiant glory and covered the throne of God, sheltered the sons of God—Adam and Eve—and sang praise to the LORD Most High. The sons of God and the Bright and Morning Star sang together at the throne. That is, until one day, iniquity was found in the heart of this beautiful angel.

He began to accuse God of being partial, unfair, and favoring the sons of God over himself. He rebelled in his heart, and his splendor faded and dulled as he could no longer reconcile why he wasn't made in the image of God as man was. Why was he not called a son of God, sharing a name with man and God? After all, he had the name of God within, didn't he? *El* was in his name, *Halel*. If we look at Isaiah 14:12 in Hebrew, where it says, "Oh, Lucifer, how you have fallen," we see that it says, *"Ek nephalta, mishamayim Halel, ben sahar:" How you have fallen from heaven, Halel, son of the morning.* It was in that moment of bitterness that he became prideful, and sin filled his heart. He had fallen,

The Mark of the Beast

and in an attempt to hurt God, he stole God's creation and took angels and men with him into his folly. He had become none other than the accuser himself: *ha-Satan*.

A very common misconception is that the "sons of God" are fallen angels. In fact, I have heard it said that the term bene *ha-elohim* is always referencing fallen angels. That's what I once thought as well.

The fallen angels are the Nephilim. Nephilim means "fallen ones" in Hebrew. There is no scripture that says that men ever fell from heaven. Ezekiel 32 does call men fallen in battle, Nephilim; I will cover this in a later chapter. Even in Genesis 3, when God cast Adam and Eve out of Paradise, it says He sent them out of the garden. It doesn't say they fell or that they were cast down or out. The only beings that are said to have been cast out or fallen from the heavens are angels. We see this time and time again in Revelation, 1 Peter, 2 Peter, Isaiah 14:12, and other scriptures.

Some believe that the Greek Septuagint is the source of understanding that denotes the sons of God as being angels because it describes the Nephilim using a word that means giants. Josephus seemed to have shared that belief as well. However, that was not the idea that was construed in the original Hebrew writings of the Torah—the Hebrew Bible.

I'm somewhat confuddled as I think about Greek mythology which describes the Titans—giant gods—that existed before the lesser gods overthrew them and took their seat of power. The Titans were giants. The demigods were typically half-god and half-animal; they were described as giants, etc. At what point did these physical giants that were part-animal become fallen angels in the folklore of the Greek civilization? It seems to me that this probably occurred circa 4th Century BC when the Jews were dispersed from Israel. In fact, the word for demon in Greek is *daimon*. The daimon in Greek mythology were living beings—demigods—that died and became *daimon*.

In the story of Hesiod's Theogony, (A Greek creation story), Zeus turneds the Titans, or Giants, into daimon at the end of the First Age. Biblically speaking, that is when the demons made their emergence on the scene. They were giants in the land until they died and became

Chapter 2: Who Are the Bene Ha-Elohim?

disembodied spirits or demons (daimon). According to Hesiod, in this time, people lived to be 1,000 years old and the land produced giant fruit and food in abundance. It is interesting how this "myth" mirrors the Bible so well. This does not prove to us, however, that the sons of God were the fallen angels. We can ascertain who the sons of God are very easily with several scriptures and understand that the giants were not fallen angels.

Let's start with Luke 3:28. The only person mentioned as a son of God in the lineage of Jesus (besides Jesus) is Adam: "Which was the son of Enos, which was the son of Seth, which was the son of Adam, which was the son of God." Adam was alive as a son of God at the time that the Nephilim chose to abandon their estates in heaven and pursue their own path. This also helps us to prove that Jesus can born a man and still be the Son of God and equal with God.

There is a prime example of this in Daniel chapter 7:

> I saw in the night visions, and behold, *one* like the Son of man came with the clouds of heaven, and came to the Ancient of days, and they brought him near before him. And there was given him dominion, and glory, and a kingdom, that all people, nations, and languages, should serve him: his dominion *is* an everlasting dominion, which shall not pass away, and his kingdom *that* which shall not be destroyed. (Daniel 7:13-14)

The word that is used here for "to serve" is *pelech* in Aramaic (Strong's 6399).[3] This word means to serve or to worship and is always used in reference to someone worshipping and serving a god of some sort.

The word for "Son of man" that is used here is *bar-enash* in Aramaic. This means the son of mortal man and refers to a human being.

What we see happening here is that a mortal man is being brought before God (the Ancient of Days), and God is making all people, tribes,

---

3. "H6399 - pəlaḥ - Strong's Hebrew Lexicon (kjv)." Blue Letter Bible. Accessed 27 Feb, 2024. https://www.blueletterbible.org/lexicon/h6399/kjv/wlc/0-1/

The Mark of the Beast

tongues, and nations worship Him as God. Since we know that God would not tell anyone to worship any God but Him, then we must assume that this mortal man, or Son of Man, is the Mashiach and is God.

The Hebrew scholar Rabbi Shlomo Yitzhaki, better known as Rashi, declared that this Son of Man was none other than the Mashiach.[4] Rashi is considered to be one of the most influential rabbinical commentators in history. To date, his teachings are still taught from an early age.

If God called Adam a son of God, and he was created, then why is it so hard to believe that He could or would beget Jesus from nothing more than a single egg in Mary? God had more DNA to work with for Jesus than He did with Adam. It is so easy for us to believe that God created Adam from dust, but for some reason, when it comes to Jesus, for many, it's just impossible for God to beget Him with no human father. Nevertheless, I digress. Hebrews 1:5-7 states:

> For unto which of the angels said he at any time, thou art my son, this day have I begotten thee? And again, I will be to him a father, and he shall be to me a son? And again, when he bringeth in the first begotten into the world, he saith, and let all the angels of God worship him. And of the angels he saith, Who maketh his angels spirits, and his ministers a flame of fire.

In fact, we read in Revelation that John falls down on the ground to worship an angel, and the angel rebukes him lovingly.

> And I John saw these things and heard them. And when I had heard and seen, I fell down to worship before the feet of the angel which shewed me these things. Then saith he unto me, see thou do it not: for I am thy fellow servant, and of thy brethren the prophets, and of them

---

4. .Chabad Lubavicht Media Center (2023, January 1). *The Complete Jewish Bible With Rashi Commentary*. Chabad.org. Retrieved October 5, 2023, from https://www.chabad.org/library/bible_cdo/aid/16490/showrashi/true/jewish/Chapter-7.htm.

Chapter 2: Who Are the Bene Ha-Elohim?

which keep the sayings of this book: worship God. (Revelation 22:8-9)

The author of Hebrews makes it clear that God never called an angel His son, therefore, they are not sons of God. Paul states in Romans 8:14, "For as many as are led by the Spirit of God, these are sons of God." (NKJV)

Now we have two criteria to meet in order to be called a son of God. You can't be an angel, and you must be doing the will of God. Those fallen angels, or Nephilim, were certainly not doing the will of God. Even the angel that spoke to John didn't put himself in the place of one deserving to be worshipped as equal with God. However, Jesus, the First Fruit, the only begotten Son of God, didn't find it to be robbery to be equal to God, according to Philippians 2:6.

Another accepted misnomer of the faith is that no one was doing God's will when the angels fell and started to attack humanity by leading them to sin. I present to you exhibit A: Cain and Abel. Cain and Abel were making sacrifices to God and providing offerings of their crops and flocks to Him. Cain was spoken to by God Himself at that time. Humanity hadn't completely turned their backs on God yet. Though humanity had sinned, they could still commune with God on a personal level.

Since they were clearly trying to be in God's favor and be accepted by Him, one can deduce that they were trying their best to adhere to God's will and thus would have been considered sons of God. For Cain, that moment ended when he succumbed to sin and murdered his brother.

Now we can look at Job 1 and 2 where it mentions the sons of God:

> One day the sons of God came to present themselves before the LORD, and Satan also came with them. (Job 1:6, NIV)

When we look at this with the rose-colored lenses we have been taught to see with by our modern theology, we understand it to be the fallen angels coming to stand before God. However, we know that this is not the case because God never calls an angel a son of God. There is

The Mark of the Beast

not just one criterion to meet to be called a son of God, there are two: being human and doing the will of God.

The word for "present themselves" is *yatsab* (Strong's 3320). It means to take one's stand—to defend oneself. This is important to understand. It tells us that the sons of God were in heaven to defend themselves, but from what or whom? They were there to defend themselves from ha-satan, the accuser. He was there to accuse them, and they were there to defend themselves against those accusations. Thank God that today we do not have to defend ourselves. Today, our Defense Attorney, our Mediator, is Jesus. In Job's time, they did not have the blessing that we do, and because of that, Satan was allowed to make a case against Job.

As we know, the qualifications for being a son of God are doing the will of God and being a human. God tells us in Job that Job was blameless. The first thing Satan did when God asked, "Have you considered My servant Job?" was accuse him. Also, take note that God called Job a servant. A servant of God does the will of God. Job then fits the criteria to be a son of God.

Now, re-read that scripture with this new lens. One day, the sons of God came to defend themselves against Satan. Those who were doing the will of God came to defend themselves against the Accuser.

It could also be that the *bene ha-elohim* was referring to Jesus in this particular scripture because *bene ha-elohim* can be singular or plural. *Benim* is the plural version of the word for "son" in Hebrew. It is taught by some rabbinic scholars that the term *bene Israel* (which is translated as sons of Israel) is more accurately translated as "son of Israel" and is referring to members of the people of Israel. So, *bene Israel* could mean that members of the sons of God were presenting themselves as individuals of a greater whole or individually. We see an example of this in Daniel 3:25:

> He answered and said, Lo, I see four men loose, walking in the midst of the fire, and they have no hurt; and the form of the fourth is like the Son of God.

Chapter 2: Who Are the Bene Ha-Elohim?

This particular passage is written in Aramaic. The portion that says the "son of God" in Aramaic reads, *lebar elohin*. In Hebrew, it would read *bene ha-elohim*. Since we see that this is clearly referring to one person, we now have a clear example of the singularity and the plurality of the *bene ha-elohim*. It also shows that the *bene ha-elohim* in Genesis 6 didn't mean every single godly human was being abominable, but members of the group known as *bene ha-elohim*.

It is possible that Job did present himself before God, and that he knew he was being attacked by Satan, and that's why he wouldn't agree with his three friends about being in sin as a viable reason for his trial. God often warns us of things that are coming, and we still question Him as to why it is happening. For example, the book of Revelation—we can't stop those events. We don't fully understand what's happening in those times, but we have an idea.

There have been times when Brandi or I have had a dream where God shows us things that are coming. We prayed against it, and it still happened. For example, I dreamed that there was a vulture that swooped down and killed a blue jay in front of me. It flew up and threatened my child, and I rebuked it. It then transformed into an eagle and flew high. Brandi knew that represented our house because we lived in a Jayco Eagle with a blue jay bird on the front. Later that week, our house was destroyed by a tornado that only touched down on our house. For the next three months, we were homeless, accused of being in sin, and had our faith tested to the limit. God forewarned us but spared us the details of what we were about to go through.

In this next part, I have added answers to several questions I often get concerning the sons of God compared to what others have taught. Since I get these questions so often, I felt that it would be beneficial to cover them in this chapter.

Question: Don't Job 1, 2, and 38 indicate that the sons of God existed before creation?

The term "sons of God" used in these verses is not before the creation of time. It is glaringly obvious that this is not the case when we read it

The Mark of the Beast

in the original Hebrew. Job 38:7 speaks of everything that was created, and then the sons of God celebrated with the Bright and Morning Star.

The Morning Star is a reference to Jesus. Genesis 2:1 records that all that was to be created was finished. "Thus, the heavens and the earth were finished, and all the host of them." The word for "host" refers to the angels and Adam and Eve. When it is translated to say *the Morning Star sang together with the sons of God*, it is speaking of man and Jesus singing together. In Revelation 22:16, Jesus says that He is the Bright and Morning Star. Job 38:7 also refers to a singular Morning Star. The plural version of "star" is used in Genesis 1:16 and that is *ha-kokabim*. There is no "im" at the end of the word *kokab* in Job 38:7, which shows it's not the normal plural construct. It is my conjecture that even though Bible Hub states that *kokab* is a plural construct, this is a mistranslation.

As we know from Revelation and 2 Peter, the Morning Star is none other than Jesus. What this verse is saying is God created the earth, and then Jesus and the sons of God celebrated with each other as one. It does not imply that any angels were celebrating God's creation, however, I think it would be a safe assumption that the angels probably did celebrate with Jesus and man. However, for this scripture, we must look at what is written plainly before us.

The next counter point is regarding what appears to be referring to the angels as sons of God in Psalm 82. We know that Psalm 82 is not speaking about angels because Jesus clearly said it was referring to human beings. We read in the book of John:

> The Jews answered Him, saying, "For a good work we do not stone You, but for blasphemy, and because You, being a Man, make Yourself God."
>
> Jesus answered them, "Is it not written in your law, 'I said, "You are gods"'? If He called them gods, to whom the word of God came (and the Scripture cannot be broken), do you say of Him whom the Father sanctified and sent into the world, 'You are blaspheming,' because I

Chapter 2: Who Are the Bene Ha-Elohim?

said, 'I am the Son of God' (*bene ha-elohim*)? If I do not do the works of My Father, do not believe Me; but if I do, though you do not believe Me, believe the works, that you may know and believe that the Father *is* in Me, and I in Him." (John 10:33-38 NKJV)

Again, even here, you see that Jesus said you can identify Him as the Son of God because He is doing the works of the Father, and by default, He is a human being.

Question: What about Numbers 13:33?

In the previous chapter, I briefly touched on the idea that the Nephilim were not the hybrid children of the angels but were in fact the fallen angels themselves. "Sons of God" here refers to the men that were formerly righteous men who partook in the fleshly sin that the daughters of Adam were partaking in.

This is nothing new. Satan has been using this tactic throughout the Bible to get righteous men to sin against God. Balaam told the king of Moab to have his people's women marry Israelites so they would sin and worship other gods, following the women. That was, as he told the king, how he would be able to curse Israel. Satan used Saul to marry his daughter Michal to David because she worshipped idols (*traphim*). And the list goes on and on throughout the Bible.

I am often asked about Numbers 13:33 (BSB), which appears to say that the descendants of Anak are the Nephilim:

> We even saw the Nephilim there—the descendants of Anak that come from the Nephilim! We seemed like grasshoppers in our own sight, and we must have seemed the same to them!

As I studied this scripture to find the truth, I came across an interesting revelation. There is a word in this passage that is not translated for some reason. However, as I look at the word in the Strong's Concordance, I see that the word is translated as "and, the, or with" (Strong's

The Mark of the Beast

854) most of the time. This word denotes closeness in proximity. With that word being translated, we get a better understanding that even the Hebrew people of Moses's time knew that the Nephilim were not the hybrid beings that were produced by the sons of God and the daughters of Adam.

Another word in this passage to take note of is the word for "came from." In Hebrew, it is one word: *min*. This word means "among" or "from among." This tells us that the Nephilim were among the descendants of Anak, or the descendants of Anak were among the Nephilim (same thing, different wording). Re-reading this verse, we now see that it says:

> We even saw the Nephilim with the descendants of Anak; Anak was among the Nephilim. We were like grasshoppers in our own sight, and we looked the same in their eyes.

Chapter 3: The Flesh of Angels and Men

The following are next in the series of questions I commonly receive regarding the sons of God. The questions require more than a simple yes or no answer, so I gave them their own chapter.

Question: Don't 2 Peter and Jude 7 point out that the sons of God sinned before the fall?

Second Peter 2:4-5 is just validation that the angels are in hell; they are not here on earth breeding and creating or perpetuating a hybrid line. The only fallen angel loosed right now is Satan, and it will be that way until the four angels are loosed from hell at the very end of days. The exact timing of when the rest of the angels were bound is not clear. I assume it may have been when Jesus commissioned the seventy disciples, because He said that He saw Satan fall from heaven like lightning (Luke 10:18). Revelation 12:8-9 tells us that Satan and his messengers lost their battle against Michael and his messengers. A place was no longer found for them in heaven, and they were cast down. It doesn't tell us exactly when that happened, but the time frame appears to be after Jesus's birth. The angels sinned, but they are denoted by Peter, who spent three years with Jesus, that they were angels and not ever did he call them sons of God.

The Mark of the Beast

Again, Jude 7 is further verification that they are not sons of God; they are angels, and they are in hell. They are never called the sons of God chained in hell. You are not a son of God if you do not do His will. Jesus states this very plainly in John 8:44 to the Pharisees who were not doing the will of God. The Pharisees believed that their traditions superseded the written law of Moses. That is why they tried to rebuke Jesus's disciples for not washing their hands before eating. That was a violation of their tradition, but it is not a written law anywhere in the Torah.

> Ye are of *your* father the devil, and the lusts of your father ye will do. He was a murderer from the beginning, and abode not in the truth, because there is no truth in him. When he speaketh a lie, he speaketh of his own: for he is a liar, and the father of it. (John 8:44)

Question: Jude 6 uses the word *oiketerion*. Isn't this the heavenly flesh body that the angels abandoned to have sex with humans and create offspring?

The heavenly dwelling we long to be clothed in, or *oiketerion*, is Jesus, and it is our resurrection flesh as well. The work *oiketerion* literally translates to "family abode" or "habitation." Romans 13:14 says:

> Instead, clothe yourselves with the Lord Jesus Christ, and make no provision for the desires of the flesh. (BSB)

Our *oiketerion* in heaven is that we actually put on the image of God the Creator, who made us to look like Him. Putting on this image is the restoration of humanity to its original design.

Second Corinthians 5:2 states, "For in this we groan, earnestly desiring to be clothed upon with our house which is from heaven." In this passage, the word for house is *oiketerion*. This translates as "family" or "family dwelling place." *Oikos* means family in Greek. Also, what Paul is talking about is putting on our resurrection body. In the verse prior, 2 Corinthians 5:1, Paul says our first house is our earthly body.

Chapter 3: The Flesh of Angels and Men

We also see a reference to this *oiketerion* in John 14:2, which states, "In my Father's house are many mansions; if *it were* not *so*, I would have told you. I go to prepare a place for you" (NKJV). The word for house is *oikia*. Again, *Oikia* is derived from the word *oikos,* which means "family." This is also where the word *oiketerion* derives its origin as well. It refers to the heavenly family, purpose, and commission; that is God's family, and it is also speaking of heaven. Heaven is God's home, and His family is heaven to Him as well.

So, the idea of it being an actual house they left is missing the key concept—the fact that "house" is referring to the family unit, not necessarily to a physical structure. Jude does mention this abode but gives a sense that they abandoned their heavenly pursuits and commissions to pursue that which is evil.

The next few verses in 2 Corinthians say: to be absent from the body is to be present with the Lord. In Greek, Paul says he is pleased to be absent from this body and be at home with the Lord. Paul further points out that while we are here in this tent, which is a temporary dwelling for our spirit, we are to act to please God.

> Therefore, we make it our aim, whether present or absent, to be well pleasing to Him. For we must all appear before the judgment seat of Christ, that each one may receive the things *done* in the body, according to what he has done, whether good or bad. Knowing, therefore, the terror of the Lord, we persuade men; but we are well known to God, and I also trust are well known in your consciences. (2 Corinthians 5:9-11, NKJV)

Furthermore, Paul clarifies that each body, whether spiritual or physical, has its own type of flesh.

> All flesh *is* not the same flesh, but *there is* one *kind of* flesh of men, another flesh of animals, another of fish, *and* another of birds.

The Mark of the Beast

There are also celestial bodies and terrestrial bodies; but the glory of the celestial *is* one, and the *glory* of the terrestrial *is* another. *There is* one glory of the sun, another glory of the moon, and another glory of the stars; for *one* star differs from *another* star in glory.

So also *is* the resurrection of the dead. *The body* is sown in corruption, it is raised in incorruption. It is sown in dishonor; it is raised in glory. It is sown in weakness; it is raised in power. It is sown a natural body; it is raised a spiritual body. There is a natural body, and there is a spiritual body. And so, it is written, "The first man Adam became a living being." The last Adam *became* a life-giving spirit.

However, the spiritual is not first, but the natural, and afterward the spiritual. The first man *was* of the earth, *made* of dust; the second Man *is* the Lord from heaven. As *was* the *man* of dust, so also *are* those *who are made* of dust; and as *is* the heavenly *Man,* so also *are* those *who are* heavenly. And as we have borne the image of the *man* of dust, we shall also bear the image of the heavenly *Man.*

Now this I say, brethren, that flesh and blood cannot inherit the kingdom of God; nor does corruption inherit incorruption. Behold, I tell you a mystery: We shall not all sleep, but we shall all be changed— in a moment, in the twinkling of an eye, at the last trumpet. For the trumpet will sound, and the dead will be raised incorruptible, and we shall be changed. (1 Corinthians 15:39-52, NKJV)

When the angels fell from their position as guardians over humankind, they may have forfeited their heavenly flesh for a different corrupted flesh; nevertheless, they are still spirit beings. This new corrupted

Chapter 3: The Flesh of Angels and Men

spirit is their new abode. It is the essence of who they have become spiritually.

Human beings were made from flesh first, then we enter into just the spirit and its flesh when we pass away. That's a great thing, such a wonderful mercy of God. If we sinned in the spirit, we would have no chance of redemption from our sin. There are no angels that are redeemed from their sin of rebellion against God. There are no sacrifices for angels that can accomplish forgiveness of their sin.

When God made man flesh first, He made a way for us to still make it to heaven. He made a way for us to be forgiven and pardoned for our sin. Even though Adam and Eve knew God face-to-face, they were still made in the flesh. They still had a chance to be forgiven.

The very first thing that God did when Adam and Eve were cast out was to make them clothing from an animal. It doesn't say that God slew an animal in order to do this, but my speculation would be that God used lamb skin to do this. I often wonder what those tunics would have looked like and how anointed they must have been to be made from the very hand of God!

I can see in the spirit clearly. I see angels, and I see demons. I can't turn it off. I'm not anyone special. I don't believe I have a special gifting or anointing at all. I have the same Holy Spirit as any other baptized believer.

When I see demons, they do look completely different than angels. Their flesh is disgusting-looking, torn, and bloody; they sometimes look like skeletons or hideous monsters. They are dark. They have no light. Sometimes they appear as though they have light or are beings of light, but it is an impure illusion. They are completely different than people in heaven and angels.

Even Satan looks different than the demons. He is a beautiful angel to this day, even though he's not as bright as he was before because he's spent so much time away from the face of God. Demonic spirits take on a different form after death, and it is very clear that they do not have the same type of spirit body as heavenly beings such as angels. Though they resemble their living selves, they are different.

The Mark of the Beast

This is what is meant by what Paul called the *oiketerion*. It's different than earth flesh, demonic flesh, fallen angel flesh, etc. Spiritual flesh, like that of angels and demons, is ethereal and cannot reproduce with the physical realm's flesh that our spirits are clothed with.

The reference to strange flesh in Jude 7 reveals the fact that human beings began to mix with animals again. Paul says, as stated in prior scripture verses I shared, that each being has its own type of flesh. Not all flesh is the same. This also shows that you cannot (or are not supposed to) mix the types of flesh. That is a command of God in Genesis 1—all types according to their own kind. This is what happens when you mix animal flesh with human flesh; your spirit takes on the form of both the man and the animal, as does your physical appearance. By this I mean that if you mix your DNA with an animal, you will look like the animal and a man, as will your seed after you. Thus, you have joined God's Spirit, which has its own spiritual body, with an animal spirit, which has its own type of spiritual body as well. All the demons I have seen are grotesque monsters. They look part lizard, part human, and all kinds of other animals, insects, fish, and all manner of weird hybrid species.

> Then shall the dust return to the earth as it was: and the
> spirit shall return unto God who gave it. (Ecclesiastes 12:7)

I will cover this more in depth in a later chapter regarding why demons are still on the earth if they are dead beings. Sounds crazy, right—humans altering flesh by adding animal DNA? Tell that to National Geographic, which reported on such experiments that had been committed in 2017. The article states:

> In a remarkable—if likely controversial—feat, scientists announced today that they have created the first successful human-animal hybrids. The project proves that human cells can be introduced into a non-human

Chapter 3: The Flesh of Angels and Men

organism, survive, and even grow inside a host animal, in this case, pigs.[5]

Taking Jude 7 to the next level requires us to look at something else that Paul said. Most people look at the phrase "strange flesh" and think it's a reference to having sex with someone. In today's culture, having sex with a new person that is not your partner is known as "strange." It is a direct, demonic reference to this verse in Jude. However, what Jude implies goes much deeper than that. The word used for "strange" in Greek is *heteras*. Strong's Concordance defines this as "altered" or "different." So, this strange flesh they were looking for was altered flesh.

In the next verse, Jude takes it a little further:

> In the very same way, on the strength of their dreams these ungodly people pollute their own bodies, reject authority and heap abuse on celestial beings. (Jude 8, NIV)

Jude uses the word *miaino* in Greek. This word means to stain, pollute, or defile. Now, knowing that the people of Sodom and Gomorrah were chasing after altered flesh, Jude uses the Greek equivalent of the Hebrew word *chalal,* which also means to pollute, stain, or defile. This shows us that to alter your flesh, or to pursue altered (genetically altered) flesh, is the same thing to God as defiling, staining, or polluting your own self. After all, what is pollution? It's the introduction of something man-made that makes an environment unsuitable or unsafe. The Antichrist and his demons are always referred to by God as animals that are unfit or unsuitable for sacrifice to Him.

If you were to go back to Genesis 14, you would see that before Sodom and Gomorrah were inhabited by human beings, they were inhabited and built by the Rephaim.

Let's look at something Paul said in Romans:

---

5. Blakemore, E. (2017, January 26). *Human-Pig Hybrid Created in the Lab—Here Are the Facts*. National Geographic. Retrieved February 22, 2023, from https://www.nationalgeographic.com/science/article/human-pig-hybrid-embryo-chimera-organs-health-science.

The Mark of the Beast

> For since the creation of the world God's invisible qualities—his eternal power and divine nature—have been clearly seen, being understood from what has been made, so that people are without excuse. For although they knew God, they neither glorified him as God nor gave thanks to him, but their thinking became futile and their foolish hearts were darkened. Although they claimed to be wise, they became fools and exchanged the glory of the immortal God for images made to look like a mortal human being and birds and animals and reptiles. Therefore God gave them over in the sinful desires of their hearts to sexual impurity for the degrading of their bodies with one another. They exchanged the truth about God for a lie, and worshiped and served created things rather than the Creator—who is forever praised. Amen. (Romans 1:20-25, NIV)

In verse 20 of this portion of Scripture, we have a time frame being established. This time frame is the foundation of the world, or creation, and a time when people began sinning against God. Simultaneously, this verse lets us know that no one has an excuse for not believing in God because all of creation was designed to reveal His glory.

The next verse we need to look at is verse 23, which says, "And exchanged the glory of the immortal God into an image made like mortal man—and birds and four-footed animals and creeping things." The word used for "exchanged" is *ellasso*. This word means to change, alter, make different, to transform. This is a very similar meaning to the word *heteras* that Jude used in his scripture; both words mean altered. This is the same word used by Paul in 1 Corinthians 15:51-52 when he talks about the rapture and how our bodies will be transformed in the twinkling of an eye.

Paul gives us a little more detail about the altering that took place. He says they altered the glory of God. Well, Jude says they sought after altered flesh. I asked the Lord, "How do I reconcile this? What am I missing?" The scripture the Lord showed me was 1 Corinthians 1:40. In

Chapter 3: The Flesh of Angels and Men

this scripture, as well as a few verses before and after, Paul is explaining that all flesh is different, whether it's animal, angel, earthly, or heavenly. He then likens that flesh to their glory. I shared this scripture earlier, but please read it here in this context:

> All flesh is not the same flesh, but there is one kind of flesh of men, another flesh of animals, another of fish, and another of birds.
>
> There are also celestial bodies and terrestrial bodies, but the glory of the celestial is one, and the glory of the terrestrial is another. There is one glory of the sun, another glory of the moon, and another glory of the stars; for one star differs from another star in glory.
>
> So also, is the resurrection of the dead. The body is sown in corruption, it is raised in incorruption. It is sown in dishonor; it is raised in glory. It is sown in weakness; it is raised in power. It is sown a natural body; it is raised a spiritual body. There is a natural body, and there is a spiritual body. And so, it is written, "The first man Adam became a living being." The last Adam became a life-giving spirit. (1 Corinthians 15:39-45, NKJV)

Paul shares here that the body has its own glory. This leads us to understand that when they altered God's glory, they altered His image, or body. Our body is made in the image of God. To alter our body is to alter His image.

Throughout the duration of Isaiah 42, God is talking about Jesus and several of the things He will carry out. Then, God even says, when speaking of Jesus:

> I *am* the LORD: that *is* my name: and my glory will I not give to another, neither my praise to graven images.

The Mark of the Beast

In this scripture, we see that God associates His name with His glory. In Hebrew, it doesn't say that He will not share his glory. It says, "I will not give My glory to another, nor My praise to idols. He is saying (paraphrased) that there won't be another Jesus—He is the only One.

The author of Hebrews states:

> And He is the radiance of His glory and the exact representation of His nature and upholds all things by the word of His power. When He had made purification of sins, He sat down at the right hand of the Majesty on High. (Hebrews 1:3, NIV)

We can determine from this scripture that Yahweh didn't say He wouldn't share His glory with anyone else. And we see that Jesus is the exact embodiment of God's nature.

This is what I believe is the blasphemy of the Holy Spirit—becoming a hybrid—because the only people who have no chance at all of repenting are those who have received the mark. They are cast into hell at the return of Jesus.

> A third angel followed them and said in a loud voice: "If anyone worships the beast and its image and receives its mark on their forehead or on their hand, they, too, will drink the wine of God's fury, which has been poured full strength into the cup of his wrath. They will be tormented with burning sulfur in the presence of the holy angels and of the Lamb. And the smoke of their torment will rise for ever and ever. There will be no rest day or night for those who worship the beast and its image, or for anyone who receives the mark of its name." (Revelation 14:9-11, NIV)

Chapter 3: The Flesh of Angels and Men

Question: What do you mean, angels don't have the anatomy to reproduce? Where does it go when you die?

That is a question I hear very often. To me, it's not much of a question at all in that angels were not created like God; only mankind was created like God. Gender is also an earth-realm thing. I believe that God, in His infinite wisdom and knowledge of the past, present, and future, knew that mankind would one day sin and no longer be allowed to remain in Paradise. Just as Satan was cast out of heaven, they would become wandering spirits. They would have no chance of redemption. Things created in the spirit don't become flesh and bone. However, as it were, man was created in the flesh with a spirit inhabiting that flesh.

When a person transitions from flesh to spirit—when they die—they can never again die a natural death. Spirit beings don't appear to be either male or female. We see evidence in Scripture that says angels don't marry, nor are they given in marriage. Also, Galatians 3:28 tells us that there is no male or female in the kingdom of God. People do, however, retain the masculine or feminine features they had on earth. By this I mean, you can tell who was male and who was female.

A man named Ron Wyatt moved on to paradise many years ago. He claimed to have found the ark of the covenant under the spot where Jesus was crucified. He took a blood sample from the mercy seat (the atonement seat in Hebrew) and had it tested in a lab in Israel. They discovered that the blood was human. He instructed the people doing the test to keep the blood at body temperature in a culture for forty-eight hours, and then to call him when they found the results so he could film it. What they discovered was mind-blowing!

The blood that was old and dried for two millennia had actually come back to life! The blood resurrected. They were able to test the DNA of the blood and discovered that it only had twenty-four chromosomes.

That is scientifically impossible because a typical human has forty-six chromosomes. They also discovered that the blood was almost entirely female except for one y chromosome that was present. When asked, "Who's blood is this?" Mr. Wyatt informed them, "It's the blood of YOUR Messiah."[6]

I find this to be of particular significance (under the assumption it is a correct and true accounting) because Jesus is referred to as the Last Adam. I believe this means that He had to be created genetically similar to Adam, and that is what the perfect human genome must have been like.

It would make perfect sense as to why there is no male or female in heaven. Your spiritual DNA becomes like Christ, who is male, but His genetic construct is more female than male.

What is most interesting to me about this is that in Genesis when God created Eve, it uses the Hebrew word that means "rib" or "one half," which would make sense because in Adam was male and female. The argument can be made that He used one-half of Adam to make her. That means that Eve was entirely consisting of Adam's DNA, but with one minor deviation—an XX Chromosome. This also shows us that the first children of Adam and Eve, though they may have looked slightly different from Adam and Eve, also had the same exact genetic construct as Adam. It wasn't until years of deviation caused by sin that we began to no longer look like Adam and Eve.

In the garden of Eden, God called Adam, "Adam." After God created Eve, God called her "Adam." They were "Adam." It was Adam that called Eve "woman." It was also Adam that named her Eve, not God. The differentiation of Adam and Eve didn't occur until the fall of man when they were escorted out of the garden by God.

Adam and Eve were not spirit beings. They were spiritual beings that had flesh bodies. I believe that the flesh they had in heaven was the same as they had on earth. If they were spirit beings in heaven, they couldn't decay or die, ever. The evidence is that Satan is not dead, and he sinned in his spirit form thousands of years ago, against the Spirit of God. Sinning against the Spirit is a truly horrendous act.

---

6. Nell, M. (2022, January 26). *Tim Mahoney interview with Mary Nell, then Ron Wyatt on the prophecies of the Ark of the Covenant.* Youtbe. Retrieved February 22, 2023, from https://www.youtube.com/watch?v=SxqXMWt-2SA&t=132s.

Chapter 3: The Flesh of Angels and Men

Each being, whether animal, human, or angel, has its own type of flesh. While talking about the diverse types of flesh, Paul says in 1 Corinthians 15:46 that the natural came first, then the spiritual. The only creatures that have flesh bodies are the ones that were created on the earth. Angels did not get flesh bodies and, therefore, cannot procreate. They only have their spirit bodies. They were not made in the image of God like we are.

Chapter 4: The Corruption of All Flesh

The word "profane" brings to mind a great deal of things when I hear it. I often imagine something profane as being blasphemous toward God, or cuss words, which are profanity. I never really stopped to question why cussing is called profanity. What does cussing have to do with blaspheming God or showing God irreverence? That is, until I started to write this chapter and study the word "profane." The knowledge that was imparted to me from this study is truly profound.

One thing that stood out to me when I originally started doing this research was that God did not destroy every creature that existed. It very specifically says in Genesis:

> And all flesh died that moved on the earth: birds and cattle and beasts and every creeping thing that creeps on the earth, and every man. All in whose nostrils was the breath of the spirit of life, all that was on the dry land, died. (Genesis 7:21-22, NKJV)

The dinosaurs were part of the hybridization that is referred to in Genesis as the corruption of all flesh.

In Genesis 6:12, it doesn't say that all mankind had corrupted their flesh alone. What it says in the literal translation from the Hebrew is:

The Mark of the Beast

"And so looked God upon the earth. For had corrupted all flesh and their way upon the earth, behold (samekh)."

Every single piece of flesh on the earth had been corrupted, except for the remnant of humans that were pure and a handful of wild beasts that were saved on the ark. Today, many people so desperately want to disprove the Bible and push their theory of evolution on the world that they disregard this scripture and say, "Why doesn't the Bible mention dinosaurs?" Allow me to answer that question in the next chapter.

The Canaanite people were well-known for sleeping with animals, as were the Greeks. The mythology of almost all the ancient world religions speaks of the gods having children with animals and creating half-human hybrid children. In fact, the word "titan" means giant, and the name Titus means "from the giants." We claim that this is just nonsense and hogwash and dismiss it, yet the Bible clearly tells us that there were human beings that had beastlike features. The very fact that God had to tell Israel not to have sex with animals is evidence that this was happening.

> Nor shall you mate with any animal, to defile yourself with it. Nor shall any woman stand before an animal to mate with it. It is perversion. Do not defile yourselves with any of these things; for by all these the nations are defiled, which I am casting out before you. (Leviticus 18:23-24, NKJV)

The word "defile," *al-tammeah*, is a variant of the same root word used to describe Noah in Genesis 6. *Tamim* in Genesis 6 means perfect, intact, pure, and undefiled in describing Noah's genetics. In the passage from Leviticus 18, there is the word "al" in front of it, which signifies "no" or "not." *Al-temmeah* means not perfect, not pure, defiled, not intact, not whole, unclean.

We can further understand that type of wholeness is referring to physical traits and attributes by researching the book of Leviticus, chapter 21.

Chapter 4: The Corruption of All Flesh

> Speak unto Aaron, saying, whosoever *he be* of thy seed in their generations that hath *any* blemish, let him not approach to offer the bread of his God. (Leviticus 21:17)

In Genesis 6:9, we see that Noah was blameless in his generations. The word used for "blameless" is *tamim*. This word is a variant of the word *mum*, which is used to mean "defect" in Leviticus. This word is the singular version in Leviticus 17, and it is the plural version in Genesis 6.

We also see the word *tamim* in Hebrew regarding sacrificial animals. And it also refers to any physical genetic defects that an animal can be born with. Understanding what the pure and spotless sacrifice meant, shows us that Noah was pure and spotless in his genetics. This word is always used in correlation with genetic defects.

In the days of Noah, something had to have happened that was creating genetic mutations which God considered blemishes that would make someone unfit for sacrifice. We know that the sacrifice that God was looking out for was the sacrifice of His Son, the Lamb of God.

Satan and his demons were causing humanity to sin against animals and interbreed with them. God said that mating with animals is what made those nations unclean that He cast out of the promised land.

These people, the Canaanites, were giants. This is a tidbit that we overlook in this verse. To be unclean, in this context, means to be impure and not intact genetically, as we just established. So, the giants were genetically impure.

You may be thinking that just means they became ceremonially unclean. Well, that cannot be the only reason that God said not to mate with animals. Mating isn't just a word that means to have sex; it also means to reproduce.

We see examples of beast-human hybrids in Genesis 14. In this chapter, we see the word *ha-zuzim*. It is used to describe a tribe of Rephaim mentioned in Genesis 14:5:

> And in the fourteenth year came Chedorlaomer, and the kings that were with him, and smote the Rephaims in

The Mark of the Beast

Ashteroth Karnaim, and the Zuzims in Ham, and the Emins in Shaveh Kiriathaim.

This word originates from the Hebrew word *ziz,* which means "beast" or "abundance." These were beast-hybrids, which means they were part animal. The word *ziz* is derived from the word *az,* meaning "goat." In all likelihood, these giants were part goat. They lived in the land of Ham, which we know is the land of Canaan, and the Canaanites were all Rephaim.

The reason I am bringing all of this up is that I found scriptures in the Bible that correlate to all this information. I am laying the foundation for a revelation that will change your entire outlook on end-time doctrine.

Let's look at Genesis 4:26 and to Seth: "To him also a son was born; and he named him Enosh. Then began men to call upon the name of the LORD." (NKJV)

At face value, this appears to be straightforward. After 238 years, men finally started to have communion with God. That was not the case, however. If humankind was not talking with God, not being righteous, not listening to His Word, not performing His will, then the prior verses in this chapter where Cain and Abel brought offerings to the Lord, and where God spoke to Cain, would contradict themselves and render that story moot.

What we see when we dig into the meat of verse 26 is a story of the origin of what would become known as the "men of renown" in Genesis 6:4.

First, let's look at the name "Enosh." Enosh means "man" and typically refers to mortal man. This is not a coincidence. God used names throughout the Bible to paint a picture of what was being done in certain time periods.

The next word we need to look at is *hu-hal* (Strong's 2490). This word is translated as "men began," but when you read the Strong's definition, it means to begin, to defile, to bore, to pierce, to profane, to begin as in opening something with a wedge, to pollute, to wound, or to cut

Chapter 4: The Corruption of All Flesh

with a sword or knife. These various meanings give us a great understanding which shows us that they began to profane something.

The word "profane" is derived from the Latin word *profanus,* which means "outside the temple." This paints a picture for us that shows not only that they were irreverent toward the name of God, but they defiled and polluted something outside the temple of God. It is my speculation that the line of Cain, and eventually whoever was a son of God that stopped following God in order to procreate with the hybrid children of Adam, profaned the outside image of the temple—that image being the glory of God or the appearance of man that was created in the image of God. One scripture that seems to coincide with this idea is 1 Corinthians 11:7. It says:

> For a man indeed ought not to cover *his* head, forasmuch as he is the image and glory of God: but the woman is the glory of the man.

The next word we need to look at is *liqro* (Strong's 7121). This word means "to call upon," but that is only the surface of understanding this word. Strong's also defines it as "to bewray oneself." Upon looking up the meaning of the word "bewray," we find that it means to speak ill of someone, to divulge. It originates from the Hebrew word *qara,* which has a wide variety of applications. Used in tandem with *liqro,* meaning to bewray, we ascertain the proper meaning of the word *liqro,* which actually means to aggressively challenge someone.

The next thing we need to understand is the word *be-shem*. Ba is a prefix that can mean of, when, in, coming, to come, in that, etc. It is a versatile prefix. *Shem,* as defined by Strong's, means name, mark, renown, memorial, a conspicuous position, or an appellation.

We see something remarkably similar to this in the book of Revelation when it speaks of the mark of the name.

> And that no man might buy or sell, save he that had the mark, or the name of the beast, or the number of his name. (Revelation 13:17)

The Mark of the Beast

We have two words to pay attention to here: *chargama* (mark) and *onomas* (name). *Chargama* is as close a word as you can get to the word *halal* in the Old Testament. It means to engrave, to stamp, to cut or carve. The purpose of this is to reshape an object in such a way that it bears the likeness of someone or something.

The best example of this is how we engrave an image on our coins. They all start as a plain piece of metal which is engraved and takes on the shape, characteristics, and form of the image it was crafted to look like. For example, an American quarter starts as a piece of silver metal. Then it is heated and stamped with a picture of George Washington. Now that quarter bears the image and likeness of George Washington.

We also see the word *onomas,* which bears a striking resemblance to the word *shem* in Hebrew. In this case, *onomas* means name, character, fame, and reputation. Stick with me. This is all-important to understanding the origin of demons.

The Hebrew mindset of the time was that someone's name was inseparable from who they were as a person. For example, in America, when we see the name, King David, we see a title and a name. David means "one who loves" or "one who is beloved." To the Hebrew mind, they would see, "King who loves," or "King who is beloved." The name not only identifies who a person is, but it also identifies their characteristics and physical and spiritual traits as well.

King David was also called ruddy, which means red. It is noted that King David had red hair. Esau was said to be born covered in hair as thick as a carpet, and he was red all over. They called him ruddy as well. Esau was a red head. This was not an uncommon trait in the days after Noah's flood. In fact, it's been discovered that some of the first pharaohs of Egypt had red hair, blonde hair, blue or green eyes, and Caucasian skin.

Just this century, the remains of a mummy discovered in 1903 were identified as those of Queen Hatshepsut. Her later ancestor, Ramses, also had red hair. They did a DNA test on Ramses and confirmed that the root of the DNA showed he was naturally born with red hair. It should be noted that Ramses did dye his hair in his old age. Nevertheless, that

Chapter 4: The Corruption of All Flesh

does not take away from the fact that his DNA showed he was a ginger. The reason I am pointing this out is simply to confirm that red hair was not an anomaly that was uncommon to the Middle Eastern regions and Africa.

Getting back on track, when you look at Genesis 4, you see that the same mark of the beast was subtly mentioned when they stated, "Men began to call on the name of God." What it says in Hebrew is, "They began to cut and pollute the image, mark, or memorial of God and profane the outside of the temple." This is the earliest known reference to the mark of the beast in the Bible.

We see this in subtle ways happening throughout the Bible as a mockery of God. What I mean by this is that when an invading army would take over Jerusalem, they would sacrifice unclean animals in the temple. They would pollute or profane the temple with the blood of an animal that was not acceptable to the Lord. This is a type of foreshadowing of the pollution of the human body with animal blood. After all, our bodies are the temple of the Lord.

Let us take a quick jump back to Genesis 6:4. The Nephilim were on the earth in those days—and afterward as well—when the sons of God had relations with the daughters of men. And they bore them children who became the mighty men of old, men of renown. One key word we must look at gives us the biggest clue that is hidden in plain sight.

While writing this chapter, I came across something interesting. What I like to do when researching Scripture is learn the translation of every single word in the verse I'm reading. There is so much fruit hidden in Hebrew words.

One rabbit trail I went down had all the possible variations of the word *laham*. This is a peculiar word that does not make it into the translation in English. This is a word that simply means "to" and "them." However, it doesn't get a Strong's translation for some reason.

Because there was no meaning given, I had to go on a quest to discover the etymology of the word. There are actually several different meanings of this word. In the context of Genesis 6:4, it means "to them."

The Mark of the Beast

It is a combination of the letter *lamed*, which means "to," and *hey mem,* which combines to mean "to them." Simple enough, right? Perhaps not.

When we dissect this word and analyze the symbolic meaning of each of the Hebrew letters, we see something interesting. Allow me to explain. The three letters used in this word are *lamed*, *hey*, and *mem*.

Hebrew letters are a type of pictograph. They all have a symbolic representation and sound associated with them. It makes sense to me that after the fall of the Tower of Babel, men would draw pictures to help them understand words and pronunciations because it helps to associate the sound of a letter or tell a story without there being a need to translate to understand each other. For example: cave paintings. We can determine what a cave painting is telling us without needing words. That same concept applies in this situation.

For this example, we're going to focus on what the original Proto-Semitic (first Semitic) alphabet meant, since that is the closest to the alphabet that Moses used when he wrote the book of Genesis.

Let's begin with *lamed*. *Lamed* was originally a symbol of a shepherd's staff. It stood for leadership and to be yoked or united together.

Next, we have *hey*. This was originally a man with his arms raised up. It stood for breath, air, spirit, and femininity. To me, this is a picture of a person surrendering to the spirit, whether good or bad.

Lastly, we have the letter *mem*. *Mem* was originally squiggly lines, kind of like a child drawing water. It stood for water, chaos, blood, and the womb. A closed *mem* stands for the inability to reproduce, while an open *mem* stands for the ability to be fruitful and multiply.

If we take the meanings of these letters in their original context, we discover that this word is implying that there was blood and chaos, men yielding to some spirit, pregnancy and birth, and being yoked or bound to something. In this case, the fact that pregnancy and birth are associated with the letters of the word tells me that there were activities such as marriage taking place. We know from reading Genesis 6:4 that this is exactly what was going on.

Chapter 4: The Corruption of All Flesh

One of the possible variants of this word has another interesting meaning as well. The word *laham* can also mean to wound, to swallow greedily, to burn, to rankle, and in some cases, to conceive. The fact that "conceive" is listed as a possible meaning is baffling to me. The word "rankle" is not a word that is used by chance either.

Rankle, when we do the word study, has quite the etymology. Rankle is Middle English: from an Old French word *rancler*. This word derived its origins from an alteration of the medieval Latin word *dracunculus*, which is the diminutive of the Latin word *draco,* or "serpent." If we re-read the tail-end part of Genesis 6:4, it reads:

> The sons of God came into the daughters of Adam, they bore them serpents (dragons); those are the mighty ones; men of the name, image, mark, or renown that polluted the outside of the temple.

This is the first time that humans mixed their DNA with serpents and beasts.

I would like to add that the word used for dinosaurs before Sir Richard Owen coined the term in 1841, was dragon. Before 1841, dinosaurs were simply known as dragons. My speculation is that if the powers that be (demons) want to hide their origins, then calling themselves by another name and coming up with a new theory of "evolution" would be a great way to do that. It is not a coincidence that "dinosaurs" typically resemble a reptilian ancestry.

Chapter 5: The Origin of Dinosaurs

The origin of dinosaurs is a topic that ties in directly with the corruption of all flesh on the earth. Many people within the body of Christ believe in evolution and that we evolved from apes or even dinosaurs. Some believe that the dinosaurs are part of a pre-adamic race that existed before Adam was created, and thus, God destroyed the earth twice. I don't buy into those theories. Here is my own theory based on Scripture.

The hidden revelation of the serpent's seed, and the possibility of some sort of carnal relations happening, as we discovered from the word "rankle," tie directly into the prophecy/curse God spoke in Genesis chapter 3 over the serpent.

> And the LORD God said unto the serpent, "Because thou hast done this, thou *art* cursed above all cattle, and above every beast of the field; upon thy belly shalt thou go, and dust shalt thou eat all the days of thy life: And I will put enmity between thee and the woman, and between thy seed and her seed; it shall bruise thy head, and thou shalt bruise his heel." (Genesis 3:14-15)

I would like to point out that most of the body of Christ looks at this scripture and has no problem believing that all the snakes in the world

The Mark of the Beast

have no legs because of the sin that was committed in the garden. We rarely stop to think that this would imply that if Satan was in fact the serpent being spoken of in the garden, then God punished all the snakes He created for the sin of an angel.

I don't believe that God would do this. He punished only the angels that fell for their disobedience, and He punished humanity for their sin. However, God doesn't punish people for other people's sins.

> The soul that sinneth, it shall die. The son shall not bear the iniquity of the father, neither shall the father bear the iniquity of the son: the righteousness of the righteous shall be upon him, and the wickedness of the wicked shall be upon him. (Ezekiel 18:20)

William Branham speculated that Eve had sex with the serpent in the garden. In English, it says that Eve was deceived. The word for "deceived" is *nasa* in Hebrew. If you go to the Strong's Concordance and look at all the possible meanings of the word *nasa*, you will find that in several instances, it means to be married or to have a desire. It is used to mean "married" 3,807 times and "desire" 5,315 times. Before this, the only mention of marriage or a wife was by Adam in Genesis 2:25, where they were both naked and they felt no shame. It is interesting how they were suddenly ashamed of their nakedness and felt as though they had to hide something in the next chapter. God had told them to be fruitful and multiply. Whether or not they had children in the garden is not mentioned, but I digress.

In Genesis 3:7, we see in English that it says, "Their eyes were opened, and they knew they were naked." I believe this may be a reference to carnal relations. I gathered this from the term later used throughout the Bible, which means "they saw or looked upon their nakedness." For example, Leviticus 18:6 uses similar wording: "None of you shall approach to any that is near of kin to him, to uncover their nakedness: I am the LORD."

Chapter 5: The Origin of Dinosaurs

Genesis 3:7 uses the word *yada* or "to know." This word can also be used to portray the act of sexual relations. Even in today's modern English, we say, "He knew his wife." That simply means they had sex.

We also see a wordplay between verse 1 and verse 7. The word for "more cunning" in Hebrew is *arum*. Then, when Adam and Eve knew each other's nakedness, we see the plural of this word *arummim*, which means nakedness. Surely it isn't a coincidence that the same word for shrewd/cunning is the same word for naked, and then the children of the woman and the serpent get cursed.

In ancient Hebrew, the phrase "to look upon or uncover their nakedness" meant to have sex with someone. We see something similar in Habakuk 2:15, which says it in a more modern manner than we see happening even today:

> Woe unto him that giveth his neighbour drink, that puttest thy bottle to him, and makest him drunken also, that thou mayest look on their nakedness!

The word for "nakedness" used in this scripture is *pudendum*. Pudendum refers to a person's exposed genitals, especially those of a female. Today, we see this played out when depraved people take advantage of someone that drank too much and passed out (to put it mildly).

I am certain the idea that looking upon someone's nakedness (exposed genitals) just means looking at them naked, is nonsense. If that were the case, according to God's law, babies would be in violation of the law because there was no formula back then. All they had was the mother's milk. I could list several reasons, but I feel this is sufficient; you can draw your own conclusions.

In each of these cases, we see the phrase "look upon their nakedness." There is no doubt that this is referring to sexual intercourse. (An interesting side note, this is the same terminology used to describe the incident between Noah and Ham when Ham "looked upon his father's nakedness.")

The Mark of the Beast

The reason I am pointing this out is because it is my speculation that Genesis 2 and 3 both allude to the fact that there was intercourse. In Genesis 2, Adam is put to sleep, and God creates Eve. God calls them *ha-adam*.

> And Adam said, "This is now bone of my bones, and flesh of my flesh: she shall be called Woman, because she was taken out of Man. Therefore, shall a man leave his father and his mother, and shall cleave unto his wife: and they shall be one flesh." And they were both naked, the man and his wife, and were not ashamed. (Genesis 2:23-25)

The author of Genesis makes it a point to distinguish that Adam and Eve were naked and unashamed. Adam even went as far as to prophesy about husbands and wives and said, "They shall be one flesh." We see in 1 Corinthians 6:16 that Paul calls sex "being united in one flesh." Jesus says the same thing in Matthew 19:5 and Mark 10:8.

I also find it interesting that Adam and Eve suddenly realize they are naked in Genesis 3 after being tempted by the serpent. This time, they know they did something wrong and shameful, and they try to cover up their sin with fig leaves. They were not ashamed of being naked before this. The part that stands out to me is that God curses the seed of the serpent and the birthing process of the woman. He curses her with pain in childbirth and then tells her that her desire shall be for her husband. The Hebrew word for "desire" used in this scripture means longing. So, God said she shall long for her husband, or yearn and desire him.

That is curious to me that God would talk about things that are related to sexual relations between a husband and a wife at a moment when all that appears to have happened is they ate fruit from a tree.

Having that theory in mind, it suddenly makes sense as to why God cursed the seed of the serpent to destruction through Jesus. If, in fact, Eve did procreate with the serpent at this point, that would explain the men of renown that are mentioned in Genesis 6:4. I will go into this in depth in the next chapter.

Chapter 5: The Origin of Dinosaurs

> And the LORD said, I will destroy man whom I have created from the face of the earth; both man and beast, and the creeping thing, and the fowls of the air; for it repenteth me that I have made them. (Genesis 6:7)

Let's look at one word that caught my attention. That word is "beast" in English, and "bahamoth" in Hebrew; this is the exact derivative of the word "behemoth" that we use in modern English.

When I think of the word "behemoth," I envision something of gigantic size and proportion. Growing up as a child, I played many games where the behemoth was always some large, dinosaur-like, dragon creature with supernatural powers. Upon inspecting that verse we see that the behemoth spoken about is most likely Leviathan, based on the revelation of Ezekiel 29, speaking of Leviathan that lives in the Nile:

> Speak, and say, Thus saith the Lord GOD; Behold, I *am* against thee, Pharaoh king of Egypt, the great dragon that lieth in the midst of his rivers, which hath said, My river *is* mine own, and I have made *it* for myself. (Ezekiel 29:3)

I would also like to point out that the men of renown, the heroes of old, these are the "man and beast" that God is talking about. These are the Greek, Mesopotamian, Egyptian, Indian, and all other cultures' gods that they tell stories about.

God said He would destroy man and beast, and creeping things, and birds of the air. He did not say man, beast, reptiles, and birds. He phrased it in such a way that shows a union of the species that He did not approve. It is my speculation that God is denoting here (Genesis 6:7) the specific creatures He would destroy. It is also my speculation that they were mixes of creatures that entailed man-and-beast hybrids and creeping things-and-bird hybrids, meaning man and the animals mixed through genetic mixing, as did birds and creeping things. The word for "creeping things" is *remes*, which means reptile or any creeping thing.

The Mark of the Beast

God did not say He would destroy all the beasts of the ground and all the birds that have life in them. If He did, and this was what He meant, then He had no right to save Noah and his wife or his sons and their wives. God would be a liar at this point because He saved seven pairs of all the clean animals (male and female), and two pairs of all the unclean animals (male and female). We know that God is not a liar, and therefore, it is safe to deduce that how we read this verse in English is not exactly how it is read in the original Hebrew.

When we look at the dinosaurs, we see a picture of exactly that. It is widely believed by evolutionists that birds descended from dinosaurs. They recently discovered that T-Rex babies were born with feathers, and they could swim because they had hollow bones like birds. Their footprints look suspiciously like that of an ostrich.

It is believed by several researchers that Velociraptors were covered in feathers and not in scales. One study noted that these *mongoliensis* raptors had quill holes on the ridges of their arms like modern birds do; these quills are meant to hold the feathers in place on a bird's wing.

If this is the case, and there was genetic mixing going on in Noah's day, then the man-beast depictions that are seen through all the ancient worlds where gods have human and animalistic traits, make perfect sense. Dinosaurs are a mix of the seed of the serpent and the other animals. I have more to say on that at another time.

Chapter 6: Nimrod's Technology

Countless generations have been captivated by the night skies. A friend of mine told me that her grandmother used to tell her that stars were little pin pricks in heaven which showed that no matter how dark the day is, heaven is always near, and it radiates light to guide all men.

Some civilizations were so enamored by space and all it held that they created star maps. They named constellations after their gods. They designed their buildings to come into alignment with certain celestial bodies, and they created holidays in honor of the solstices. I often pondered why the extreme obsession with stars and space, until one day, my eyes were opened by a simple statement from a soon-to-be friend.

The first thing we must show is the period that Jesus refers to as "the days of Noah." Noah was still alive when Abraham was born; he was alive during Nimrod's reign also. So, when Jesus says, "as in the days of Noah," He is not specifically only referring to the pre-deluge era, but to Nimrod and Abraham's time simultaneously.

I had the opportunity to do an interview with Ivan Tuttle. Ivan died and went to hell, and then he was taken to heaven. He got to see the beginning of time to the end of days while he was there. One thing that he shared with me was that in Nimrod's time, just 120 years after the flood (approximately), they were already able to travel to space further than we have been able to, even today. That

The Mark of the Beast

got the old noodle thinking. I started to do research on the fact that there could have been technology at that time.

I read in one extra-biblical account of the Genesis time that a man spoke about angels coming to earth and sharing advanced mathematics, witchcraft, astronomy, astrology, etc. When we look at the pre-diluvian cities (meaning built before the flood), we see evidence that the civilizations of the world shared common knowledge of these topics. The buildings line up with equinoxes; they were able to accurately track the length of days, weeks, months, and years, and even incorporate their knowledge into the structures themselves.

In the days of Nimrod, people all shared one language. All the tribes of humans were related. They had fallen angels giving them advice, teaching them witchcraft, sharing advanced mathematics, teaching them astrology, leading them into sexual sin, and every sinful thing they could, just as they were doing before the flood. The single language they spoke was a derivative of the language of heaven. Can you imagine having access to a language that is directly derived from heaven? That would be like being able to speak in tongues all the time and always having that access to the spiritual realm. I believe that the language spoken on earth at that time had probably changed significantly in the 1,600 years it existed from Adam and Eve to the great deluge, much like English has progressed from a purely Germanic language to the English we know today.

It's important to understand that the angels that fell and gave spiritually illegal knowledge of heavenly things to men, had special skills. In Ezekiel 28:17, we can gain some understanding into this type of "wisdom" and knowledge that was bestowed.

> Thine heart was lifted up because of thy beauty, thou hast corrupted thy wisdom by reason of thy brightness: I will cast thee to the ground, I will lay thee before kings, that they may behold thee.

Chapter 6: Nimrod's Technology

The word for "wisdom" used here is *chokma*. The Jewish concept of *chokma* is different from the American idea. *Chokma* is a type of wisdom that includes skill, knowledge, experience, and the ability to perform a task. When God was giving the blueprints to the Israeli people to create the items for the tabernacle and the Temple, He gave the metal workers the *chokma* or skill (wisdom) to be able to create things according to the exact specifications He appointed.

When the angels gave mankind their secret "wisdom," it was part of the skill set they operated in and were given by God. They knew how something worked in heaven and how to make that same thing happen here on earth. It is my opinion that, in exchange, they traded their knowledge and heavenly skill for mankind's allegiance and worship to them rather than to God. That is the trafficking referred to when the Bible says Satan corrupted his sanctuaries by the multitude of his iniquities and the dishonesty of his trading:

> Thou hast defiled thy sanctuaries by the multitude of thine iniquities, by the iniquity of thy traffick; therefore will I bring forth a fire from the midst of thee, it shall devour thee, and I will bring thee to ashes upon the earth in the sight of all them that behold thee. (Ezekiel 28:18)

Many people have scoffed at the notion of mankind having advanced technology eons ago. However, I must point out how amazing humankind is. Look at what we have done as human beings in the last 150 years with several languages and no angels sharing the things that they shared with the first humans. We went from horse and buggy, primitive firearms, no electricity, etc. Now, in 2024, we can use an app to translate any language. We have satellites traveling all through space. We have humans living in space. Soon we will have people living on Mars. We have cars, airplanes, nuclear bombs, computers, cures for all kinds of diseases, etc. All of this technology sprang up within 150 years. Mankind's ability to grow and advance is unprecedented.

The Mark of the Beast

Now, let's get into the scripture behind my theory of technology in the ancient days. Genesis 11:3 says, "Then they said to one another, 'Come, let us make bricks and bake *them* thoroughly.'" They had brick for stone, and they had asphalt for mortar.

I did a little word study on this sentence and discovered that the word for bricks is derived from the word *laban* and means white. They were making white bricks and sealing them with bitumen. I did a little more research at the behest of the Holy Spirit and discovered that when the pyramids were finished, they were shiny and white. I also learned that their stones were sealed together with bitumen.

In the genealogy of Ham, we learn that Egypt (Mizraim in Hebrew) was born around the same time as Nimrod. The post-flood era was approximately 4,200 years ago, or around 2,500-2,400 BC. In Seti's tomb, which is believed to be about 1,000 years later, hieroglyphs were discovered of a helicopter and a flying machine or space craft of some sort.

This time frame is when the hybrids began to re-emerge. The first hybrid to surface post-flood was Nimrod himself. There is no mention of hybrids being before Nimrod from Ham's genealogical line, which shows us that neither Ham nor his wife were part hybrid, nor was Noah. If they were, then all their kin would have been hybrid as well, and that would include us. And we know that Noah was perfect in his generations.

I believe that Nimrod was manipulating himself to become a *gibborim*. *Gibborim* is the Hebrew word for a mighty man. In the book of Genesis, this word was used to describe the hybrid offspring of the dragon's seed and the seed of man. It literally translates as "mighties," or as we would say, "mighty ones." This word would eventually come to mean men who were great warriors in battle. I believe that when it says he pierced (became) a *gibborim*, it is showing that he was performing some sort of surgery or genetic alteration by taking the flesh of dead dinosaurs, perhaps the bone marrow of an animal, and inserting it into himself.

Chapter 6: Nimrod's Technology

You think that's crazy, right? Is that not even possible? Well, just a short while ago, a man got a bone marrow transplant, and his DNA changed to become the DNA of his donor. A few months after his bone marrow transplant, they swabbed his cheek and discovered the DNA of his donor in his saliva. A few years after that, they tested his semen to discover that his DNA had been so affected by his transplant, that his semen no longer shared his DNA but was the DNA of his donor as well. There is evidence that the first cranioplasty, which is when you replace deformed parts of a skull with some other material, was performed over 6,000 years ago. There are skulls of hybrids that were DNA tested and shown to be descended from the Middle East, discovered in Paracus, Peru, dating back to 0 AD—approximately the year Jesus was born—that had successfully had part of their skull replaced with a gold plate, and it had healed with bone growth around the plate. With these amazing medical advances in light, it's not really that hard to imagine that about 4,000 years ago, people could very well have been tampering with genetic altering.

There are two arguments that have most commonly been presented to me about this theory. The first is that science speculates the pyramids were built by the Egyptians before the time of the flood, according to modern academia. The issue I have with this is that the Bible clearly details that Mizraim (Egypt) was born around the same time as Nimrod. In fact, Egypt was the uncle of Nimrod. Nimrod and Egypt are detailed as being born after the flood in Genesis 10. The Bible is right and true, and all else that contradicts the Word of God is false.

The second argument I hear is, "Well, why is there no sign of the technology you're talking about after the Tower of Babel? Why did they go back to the stone age?"

That's a good question. You must understand that when the languages were confounded, no one was able to speak to one another. Everyone had to start from scratch and learn to communicate again. There were, however, some that escaped to space. In my mind, it makes sense why the first forms of writing were pictographs. I can't

The Mark of the Beast

think of a much easier way to display a message than drawing a picture to stand for a word or a sound.

The evidence of this technology is quite clear when you look at the ancient religions. Nearly every religion has an accounting of the tale of the flood in some form. Most of the Native American tribes in the Americas have stories about giants that lived in the land—in the mountains—and ate human beings.

With the advancement of this technology, I believe that Nimrod and several of his cohorts were altering human DNA to produce and transform themselves and the world into a new species of hybrids that were genetically engineered.

> Come, let us build ourselves a city, with a tower that reaches to the heavens, so that we may make a name for ourselves; otherwise, we will be scattered over the face of the whole earth. (Genesis 11:4, NIV)

When we break this down in the original Hebrew, we see that it says, "Let us make for ourselves a tower." The word for tower is *va-migdal*. This word means "tower" or a "pyramidal-shaped bed of flowers." Right there, I see the pyramids, and I am reminded of the fact that Mizraim was a relative of Nimrod, and they built the pyramids.

The fun doesn't end there, however. The next verse alludes to the fact that these people were building a tower to send men into space. This sounds like a cockamamie tale but bear with me. They said, "Let's build a tower (a reference to pyramids) whose top reaches the heavens." The word used in Hebrew that is translated "the top" is not the word top, which is *rosh*. This word is a derivative of *rosh*, and it is *varoshov*. It means a captain or company (group of men). Then obviously, *ba-shamayim* means heavens or in space.

I am not saying that I think the pyramids were the Tower of Babel. I do, however, feel it's a vital component to take note of. We see pyramidal structures built all around the world in one form or another, most of which stem from the same time frame as the Tower

Chapter 6: Nimrod's Technology

of Babel, and they appear to have been created using advanced mathematics, knowledge of solstices, astronomical alignment, and even in the case of Mayan cities in Mexico and Egypt, they are laid out in the shapes of the constellations they observed in their area of the world.

The pyramids of Egypt are located at 29.9792458 degrees north, which directly mirrors the speed of light. The dimensions of the pyramids are measured in what appear to be metric increments. The size of the pyramids is 1:43200 scale to the earth's dimensions. The golden ratio is found in the dimensions of the pyramid as well as Pi. In my mind, this is not just a coincidence. This is a demonstration to the world that they were advanced beyond what archaeologists assume to date.

Getting back on track, next we read, "And let us make for ourselves a name, lest we be scattered abroad." The word for name is *"shem."* However, given the information in the earlier chapters, we know that word can mean name, mark, image, or memorial. I believe this is showing that they wanted to create their own image and once again profane the name of God by mixing their flesh with animal flesh. Thus, the second mark of the beast was established. As we see in Jude 7, the Rephaim had altered flesh. Again, how crazy is it to believe that they were using genetic alterations in 2,400 BC when even the Bible says that they were altering their flesh? To me, if you can find it in the Bible, then it's only as silly to the extent you believe in the complete validity of the Bible.

We can read Genesis 11:4 more clearly as: "Let's build a tower with a company of men that reaches the heavens (space)." Couple this with the following scriptures:

> Though they dig into hell, thence shall mine hand take them; though they climb up to heaven, thence will I bring them down. (Amos 9:2)

The Mark of the Beast

> Though thou exalt thyself as the eagle, and though thou set thy nest among the stars (*kokawbim*), thence will I bring thee down, saith the LORD. (Obadiah 1:4)

> Warriors are coming from a distance and from the ends of Heaven, LORD JEHOVAH and the weapons of his wrath to destroy all the Earth (Isaiah 13:5, ABIPE)

It seems to me that the hybrids were traveling through space for an exceptionally long time, though now, things are escalating and accelerating. Theoretical interdimensional travel and quantum entanglement make this possible, but I will have to explain that in depth in a future book. The scripture is there, the reference is in Genesis, and the Lord will use these hybrids to bring about the end-of-days Antichrist scenario. This gives us a clearer understanding of what Jesus was saying when he said, "As in the days of Noah."

I know what you're thinking: ancient astronaut theorist here, round earther, ridiculous, etc. We will delve more into this later, but evidence that these hybrids and humanity were in space is clear in the written accounts of ancient peoples and their mythos. Every civilization has a myth about how humankind came from heaven in some kind of ship and started altering humans to make them "gods." The sad truth is that there are reports of "aliens" telling people that this is what they have been doing. This has also become part of the mainstream extra-terrestrial phenomenon.

The devil uses the same tricks repeatedly. He hasn't done anything new. If you think he has any new tricks, read Hebrews 4:15:

> For we have not an high priest which cannot be touched with the feeling of our infirmities; but was in all points tempted like as *we are, yet* without sin.

If Jesus was tempted the same way we are, so He knows exactly what we are going through, and that is still true today, then we can logically deduce that Satan isn't doing anything new.

Chapter 6: Nimrod's Technology

Since Satan isn't doing new things, we can expect that what he was doing in the past will be repeated. That means if the Bible is telling us they had the ability to travel through space, then that is what we will see.

I believe that not everyone had this type of technology. It appears to have begun in the Middle East. This assertion aligns with the Bible in that Nimrod was the leader of this rebellion, and his kingdom was in the Levant. The Levant is the term used to describe the geographic area in Middle Eastern Europe that encompassed Israel, Jordan, Lebanon, Syria, and that general area. Levant means "to rise" in French and implies that it is in the direction of the eastern sunrise, which directly relates to the position of this land being east of France.

Humankind had spread and did not all share the same pursuits. Some were still living primitive lifestyles and hadn't seen any of this advanced technology. If you look at the hieroglyphs of the period in which Nimrod existed, you will see that the giants and the ones depicted as having technology were always described as forcing those without that technology—those that were human—to be their slaves.

On the other hand, all the world could have had this technology. We can't rule that out entirely. It is believed that in the event of a global disaster such as a nuclear war, large coronal mass ejection (CME), an attack on infrastructure using an electromagnetic pulse, or a massive earthquake that shakes the entire world, etc., that it would only take about 120 years—four generations—for mankind to forget how to manufacture and use that technology. Within those 120 years, men would revert to living like they did in the Stone Age, having to redevelop civilization yet again. There may be some signs of the technology left, some random vestiges here and there, but, without the proper education and understanding of that technology, it couldn't withstand or be maintained.

This is an interesting idea since Abraham was born a mere 140-200 years after the catastrophic events of Nimrod's time, and there is no mention of technology that we are aware of in his time. That

The Mark of the Beast

is, at least not any that hasn't been deliberately obfuscated by the global government. Could that be the truth, or is it what we are supposed to believe? I'll leave that for you to ponder. Meanwhile, let me help persuade you.

I discovered that there are several hieroglyphs in Egyptian tombs that portrayed light bulbs, airplanes, and even a helicopter. Some are in the tomb of Seti. Some are in the tomb of Hathor. In parts of ancient Mesopotamia several devices were discovered that are believed to have been batteries and even a device used for electroplating gold onto other metals.

Another striking occurrence is that NASA discovered a face of a sphinx on Mars, a building that looks like a pyramid capstone, Egyptian tombs, and even statues resembling those of Egypt. Many dismiss this as pareidolia, meaning we want to see it, therefore, we see it—like when you look at a cloud and see an animal, but no one else does. It's just a cloud. It is not a coincidence that the Bible subtly depicts the ties between Egypt and the Tower of Babel and space travel, and we see photos of Egyptian-looking "rock formations" found on the face of Mars. Surely this isn't just a coincidence.

I also discovered there are Hindu texts from the approximate period of Nimrod, called the Vadas. These books detail complicated surgeries, such as brain surgery, and machines that could fly using electromagnetic mercury ion-powered engines (Vimana).

One of these Vimana crafts was reconstructed in the late 1800's by a man named Shivkar Talpade. He built an aircraft that used a mercury-powered electromagnetic motor that was based on the instructions of the Vimana. It was reported to have flown up to 1,500 feet (about 457.2 meters) before coming down. The official story is that this never happened, and it was a lie, etc. But there are pictures out there that were taken of this ship in the air, flying.

The reason I am pointing all of this out is that this information all points back to around the same time that Nimrod was alive. He was a wicked king. There is much hidden between the lines concerning Nimrod. According to Josephus, Nimrod was the one responsible

Chapter 6: Nimrod's Technology

for trying to unite the world, and he wanted to seal buildings with bitumen in an act of defiance, so if God did decide to flood the world again for the sin they were committing, they would be flood proof.

Through the rapid advancement of their technology, they became haughty and arrogant. They thought they had become gods and could strike God in defiance. This was truly a wicked generation.

That defiance in the face of God is what would inevitably lead to the destruction of the Tower of Babel, the splitting of the continents—which they were trying to prevent—and the scattering of all people and languages.

Chapter 7: The Division of the Continents

The world was in rebellion. They corrupted the image of God, laughed in His face, and defied Him—even though they had first-hand knowledge of the flood that destroyed the people of the world who had sinned only a century before them.

Nimrod wanted to unite the world. He wanted to be a king and a god. In fact, many believe that he became the god, Ba'al. He knew that he was in sin, and he devised a scheme to save his own skin. But, inevitably, it would all be for nothing.

Let's take a jump back to Genesis 10:25 (this is still dealing with the days of Nimrod).

> And unto Eber were born two sons: the name of one was Peleg; for in his days was the earth divided; and his brother's name was Joktan.

The Hebrew word for "divided" is *Nipalag*. This is a combination of two words: *Ni* and *Palag*. *Ni* means simply "I" in Hebrew. *Palag* means to split, divide, or cleave. This word is unique in the fact that it refers to something being torn down the middle. In Genesis 11:8, we see that God scattered the people abroad and confused their language.

The Mark of the Beast

> So the LORD scattered them abroad from thence upon the face of all the earth: and they left off to build the city.

It is commonly believed that, at this time, God separated the people because He did not want them all meeting together in one place. You see that the Canaanites—Nimrod and his cohorts—were worried that the people would spread across the land and be divided. I say Nimrod because the Tower of Babel was built in the plain of Shinar, which was part of his kingdom.

These people knew that they were in sin and in blatant defiance of God because Scripture shows us that they were planning to build a tower that was sealed with bitumen, just like Noah's ark was. The reason God had Noah seal the ark with bitumen was because it would waterproof the ark.

The people in the time of Nimrod knew that they were going to face judgment for what they were doing, and that is a different level of sin. This takes your average blasphemy and turns it into super blasphemy.

They were trying to spare themselves from the wrath of God and His judgment they knew they were incurring, so they were building a waterproof tower to protect themselves from a possible flood. In all reality, there was probably a good amount of flooding that occurred during the time the Tower of Babel was destroyed by God.

In 1 Chronicles and Genesis 10, we see in the accounting of the bloodlines of Noah's sons that the earth was divided or split apart. God told Moses that He divided—cleaved—the earth by splitting it. This split was God separating the nations. Moses specifically pointed out in Genesis 10:16-18 that the tribes of Canaanite descent were scattered all over the face of the earth (abroad).

If you look at maps of what the primal continent, Pangea, as we know it today, looked like, you will notice that South America and North America are west of Europe and Africa. I believe that these Canaanite tribes were dispersed among North America and South America.

Just a few paragraphs before, I mentioned that the descendants of Phut were noted as being west of Egypt, and I proposed that they were

Chapter 7: The Division of the Continents

most likely (in my opinion) twins. The Egyptians had several red-haired mummies and several mummies that have elongated skulls. Recently, several mummies with elongated skulls, six fingers and toes, gigantic stature, and red hair were found in Paracus, Peru, and in Iraq. In several parts of North America including New York, Massachusetts, Vermont, California, Arkansas, and other states, skeletons averaging nine to fourteen feet or taller were found inside colossal burial mounds. Some of these skeleton's legs alone were five feet long.

As I said before, Egyptian mummies had red hair, blonde hair, and black hair. What is interesting is that the mummies found in Peru had red hair as well. According to the modern theory of evolution, that should not exist because the Europeans did not come to the Americas until the 1400s (that can be proven anyway). I believe that the Canaanite tribes that were spread abroad were the progenitors of these South American and North American giants. When I say, "spread abroad," what I mean is that these are the remnant of the Canaanite people that had already spread widely throughout the earth before the continents were divided. These people were then cut off from their Middle Eastern families because of the great divide we now know as the ocean (though I believe the Canaanite tribes did migrate about 1,000 years after the flood as well, which I will cover later in this book).

Many have stated that it's scientifically impossible for God to have split the continents at the time of the Tower of Babel. They say it would have caused a massive flood on the earth, and all the inhabitants would have died. Even if the world was flooded, they would have all had the knowledge to build a boat at that time. Not all humans would have been destroyed. If they were smart enough to waterproof their buildings, surely, they would have gathered supplies in preparation for God's wrath. Mankind has not changed very much in 6,000 years. There are still people trying to protect themselves from God's wrath by building bunkers and storing supplies.

I do not find this assertion to be biblical. If we look at the book of Revelation, we see something that blows this theory of humanity perishing in a continent-dividing earthquake, out of the water.

The Mark of the Beast

> And there were voices, and thunders, and lightnings; and there was a great earthquake, such as was not since men were upon the earth, so mighty an earthquake, *and* so great. And the great city was divided into three parts, and the cities of the nations fell: and great Babylon came in remembrance before God, to give unto her the cup of the wine of the fierceness of his wrath. And every island fled away, and the mountains were not found. And there fell upon men a great hail out of heaven, *every stone* about the weight of a talent: and men blasphemed God because of the plague of the hail; for the plague thereof was exceeding great. (Revelation 16:18-21)

From these scriptures, we see that the earth was shaken so severely that the islands and mountains disappeared. This is a shaking that is worse than the separation of continents in the days of Babel—enough to put the entire world, or at least various mountains, under water. However, mankind doesn't completely disappear off the face of the planet. In fact, they shake their fists at heaven for God doing such a thing.

When reading the Bible, we cannot dismiss the supernatural ability of God to do something that doesn't make sense to our human minds or our lower logic. God can make man from dirt. He can make man from a female with no sperm. He SPOKE the universe into being. It is not impossible for Him to divide continents without flooding the world.

That was quite the rabbit trail! Let's get back on course. If you look at the Clovis people of America, it was recently discovered that a 19,000-year-old (or so we're told that's the age) flint knife was discovered in Virginia in 1971. The spectacular aspect of this knife is that the material originated in France. Archeologists believe that somehow Europeans migrated to America 19,000 years ago. However, if you put the continents back together, forming the ancient Pangea, you will discover that Virginia was only a few days journey from France at one point.

In western Oklahoma, cave paintings were discovered in an ancient Celtic language, along with Egyptian hieroglyphics that had no business being there. It is deemed, "the cave of Anubis." It puts them at a time

Chapter 7: The Division of the Continents

when no European had supposedly traveled to America, according to modern history.

The latest scientific evidence and theory of the extinction of these giant races in the Americas, is that they inbred themselves so much that they died off. Incest is a trait that was common to the Canaanite people. In fact, it was so common that the Lord gave a law to the Hebrew people, telling them: do not be like them; do not mate or breed with animals and defile yourselves the same way they did; don't sleep with your sister or mother, etc.

In Egypt, it was quite common for direct family members, such as siblings, or mother and son, to marry. The Egyptians believed this preserved the blood of the gods that was in their lineage. Therefore, you see examples of rulers like King Tut, who had several genetic deformities that resulted from direct incestual childbearing.

If, in fact, these people are descendants of the Canaanite tribes, then it would make sense that they shared the same moral values as their predecessors. Evidence of their common ancestry is seen throughout the world.

Several Native American and South American tribes, such as the Choctaw, Chickasaw, Pauti, Manta, and Natchez, tell of a race of white giants that cannibalized them, were ten feet tall or more, built strongholds and giant cities, and had superior mining skills. They inhabited the land when the Native Americans migrated west, and the Natives fought and killed them at every chance they could. The Pueblo people have cave paintings and traditions of their people coexisting with these giants having six fingers and toes.

Some of these tribes of hybrids didn't come to the Americas until some 1,000 years after the time of Nimrod. This is shown by places like the American Stonehenge in New England. This amazing building had an inscription written on it that reads, "This temple is to Ba'al of the Canaanites, this dedication." This has no business being in America nearly 2,000 years before Christopher Columbus discovered the "West Indies." This inscription was found at America's Stonehenge in Salem, New Hampshire.

The Mark of the Beast

There have also been other places discovered in America that have such out-of-place artifacts. A Native American chief of the Nez Perce, named Chief Joseph, had in his possession a receipt of sorts that had Assyrian cuneiform written on it. Chief Joseph explained that it was a family heirloom that had been passed down for generations. He said it was given to him by his white ancestors who taught them many things.

This shows me that, at some point, the hybrids did begin to travel from their native lands in the Middle East and head to the Americas in a great diaspora. The reason I hypothesize this is the case is because the Iberian Punic script is a post-flood language. The date on the monument is around 1,000 BC, but the flood happened around 2,400 BC. That's a 1,000-year time difference from the days of Noah to the period that Joshua was heading into the promised land and slaying the remnant of hybrid-giants that occupied the land. I do not believe this is just a coincidence.

Chapter 8: The Biblical Origin of Demons

Now that we have established that hybrids were found across the entire world, let's talk about why they would be demons. There is one major premise on which I will base this next chapter—my hypothesis, if you will. All demons are the disembodied spirits of the giants: Anakim, Rephaim, or any other name describing these hybrid humans. Again, they are not fallen angels.

I can hear it now: "Um, all humans that die go to heaven or hell; there is no in-between." You would think that was entirely the case. Scripture shows that Satan is not in hell, yet it says that the rest of the angels that fell are chained in hell. You should also consider that hybrids are not fully human; they are part beast.

When we look at Matthew 8:28-29, we read:

> When He had come to the other side, to the country of the Gergesenes, there met Him two demon-possessed *men,* coming out of the tombs, exceedingly fierce, so that no one could pass that way. And suddenly they cried out, saying, "What have we to do with You, Jesus, You Son of God? Have You come here to torment us before the time?" (NKJV)

The Mark of the Beast

It is interesting that even the demons can identify the Bene ha-Elohim.

First, let's look at one subtle thing the demons said, that we often overlook: "Have you come to torment us before the time?" The Greek word used for "time" here is *kairos*. This word means "happening at exactly the right or most opportune time." This seems meaningless and as though it is just trivial banter, but they are asking Jesus if He is going to sin against God and torment them.

The word for torment means to be tortured, to be tossed to and fro like a wave that travels in a circular, buffeting manner. This is evidence that they know their fate is going to parallel Revelation 20:10:

> And the devil, who deceived them, was thrown into the lake of burning sulfur, where the beast and the false prophet had been thrown. They will be tormented day and night for ever and ever. (NIV)

The same word used in Matthew 8 for torment is used here in Revelation 20. The demons know their fate. Somehow, the book of Revelation was not a surprise to them.

We see in 2 Peter 2:4, as mentioned above, that the angels are already in hell and chained with chains of gloomy darkness. There is no mention of any angels being loosed from any chains except in Revelation 9:14 when only four angels that are bound under the Euphrates River are loosed to destroy one-third of the population. Currently, that would be approximately 2.3 to 3.3 billion inhabitants of the earth.

This is carried out and found more clearly in Genesis 14 by the various names and descriptions of the Rephaites (Rephaim in Hebrew); Zuzimites (ha-Zuzim, meaning beasts, which is derived from the word *az*, meaning goat—goat-man in Hebrew), the terrors (ha-emim); the builders (Kiriathim); the Horites (cave dwellers—people who built homes in caves and crevices like a serpent burrows into a wall or crack). We will get into this a little bit more, but here is a taste.

Those who built their dwellings in caves and mountainsides are seen in North and South America as well as in the land of Canaan.

Chapter 8: The Biblical Origin of Demons

There is a city in Derinkuyu, Turkey, that dates back 4,000 years and is entirely underground. Interestingly enough, 4,016 years ago is when it is believed the Tower of Babel was constructed.

In Peru, skeletons of giants have been discovered with long necks and eyes that are approximately one-third larger than human eyes, indicating they could see at night in the dark. All of that was discovered by none other than L.A. Marzulli with his diligent research into the obfuscated history of the world.

Another theory that people like to speculate about is that the current land of the Canaanites is inhabited by the original people who settled there. But Scripture teaches us that Egypt, Ethiopia, Libya, and the Middle East were occupied by the Rephaim hybrids.

Deuteronomy 2:10-12 states:

> The Emim had dwelt there in times past, a people as great and numerous and tall as the Anakim. They were also regarded as giants, like the Anakim, but the Moabites call them Emim. The Horites formerly dwelt in Seir, but the descendants of Esau dispossessed them and destroyed them from before them, and dwelt in their place, just as Israel did to the land of their possession which the Lord gave them. (NKJV)

As stated previously, a large portion of the mummies and skeletons that have been found in this area have had red hair. Esau was a red head. One mummy was a pharaoh that had red hair and white skin.

In Caral, Peru, which was built approximately 4,000 years ago, the city very much mirrors the pyramidal structures seen in Egypt that were constructed during the same period.

There is even speculation that a sizable number of people that inhabited the Middle East were white, blond-haired, blue-eyed, Nordic-looking people called the Ammonites. If you were delving into that tangent, you would discover a race of beings called the Aryans, who are the basis for Hitler's Holocaust. That's a rabbit hole we will avoid!

The Mark of the Beast

As you get closer and closer to the Fertile Crescent, you notice that there is increased reference to ancient technology that existed in the time of Nimrod. As these civilizations developed, they branched out westward and eastward, which is the depiction of the dispersion of the tribes in Genesis 10-11.

Psalm 91 refers to demonic forces that cannot harm you under the shadow of God's wings:

> You will never worry about an attack of demonic forces at night nor have to fear a spirit of darkness coming against you. (Psalm 91:5, TPT)

> I will send my terror ahead of you and throw into confusion every nation you encounter. I will make all your enemies turn their backs and run. (Exodus 23:27, NIV)

The word used for terror here is *emati*, which is the same variant of the word used to describe the Emim giants in Genesis 14:6. Interestingly, the word used in Genesis 14:6 is specifically used in Job as well:

> It is drawn, and comes out of the body; Yes, the glittering point comes out of his gall. Terrors come upon him. (Job 20:25, NKJV)

The word is very specifically *Emim*. These terrors, or the terror by night, are the *ha-emim* spirits.

Each of these different tribes of hybrids descended from Ham, the son of Noah. Ham's son Canaan was cursed by Noah after Ham sinned against him a year after the flood. This sin that was committed was an incestual rape of Noah by Ham. I will now re-share some scriptures from before to reiterate and remind you, the reader, of what was previously shown about "seeing their nakedness" in the time of Noah.

The Hebraic language had a very polite way of saying "roofied" or "date rape" or "to have sex with," in the time of Moses. The phrase

Chapter 8: The Biblical Origin of Demons

they used was, "to look upon their nakedness." You see this in Leviticus 18:7, which we more accurately translate today to read:

> Do not dishonor your father by having sexual relations with your mother. She is your mother; do not have relations with her. (NIV)

In Hebrew, it says, "Do not look upon the nakedness of your father or the nakedness of your mother, for she is your mother, do not look at her naked, she is your mother, you shall not uncover her nakedness."

Habakkuk paints this picture for us by saying:

> Woe to him who gives drink to his neighbor, pressing him to your bottle, even to make him drunk, that you may look on his nakedness! (Habakkuk 2:15, NKJV)

In this light, you can easily see why Noah was enraged when he woke up from his drunken stupor and cursed Canaan, his fourth grandson from Ham, after the flood.

The reason this is important is because this is where sin and defilement crept into the seed of man again. This was not where the giants came from, resulting in the second incursion of hybrid giants, but it is how the Enemy was able to attack humankind in the future.

Canaan was the great-grandson of Noah and the grandson of Ham. Ham's children were evil, and there is no mention that Ham ever repented of raping his father. Without repentance, the children are left vulnerable to the generational curse as a result. This also left them susceptible to sin and demonic influence because Ham was not righteous and did not teach his children to be righteous.

Some have conjectured that either Noah or his wife were part hybrid, but remember, Genesis 6:9 says that Noah was blameless in his generations. The word translated as "blameless" means complete, untouched, unblemished, pure, whole, intact, perfect, without defect. When it says that Noah was blameless, it indicates that he was in no way mixed with

The Mark of the Beast

the hybrid genetically. He was spotless, complete, intact, pure, and perfect in his genetic composition.

Again, if either Noah or his wife were hybrids, all of humanity today would be hybrids. If Noah was a hybrid, then you and I would be hybrids and not able to be saved, which we know is not true. The hybrids are always noted as being evil, wicked, practicing evil, and totally hating God. They also have identifying markers like extra rows of teeth, extremely tall height, extra fingers or toes, long necks (Anakim), beast-like characteristics, and so on.

God refers to hybrids as being corrupted after he says Noah is blameless. This word for "corrupt" means spoiled.

> So God looked upon the earth, and indeed it was corrupt; for all flesh had corrupted their way on the earth. (Genesis 6:12, NKJV)

In Hebrew, this translation says:

> And God looked (using the plural form to represent the Trinity; Elohim) on the earth and indeed it was corrupted; for it had corrupted all flesh and their way on the earth.

Take note that God declared all flesh was corrupt, and their way, or walk in life, was corrupt as well. If He was only referring to the people being wicked in their heart, then He had no reason to identify that their flesh had been corrupted or spoiled as well.

If you look at the genealogical line of Ham, you will notice factions that occurred where flesh had been corrupted and produced hybrids again. The most obvious are the Cushites, the Mizraim (Egyptians), Phut, and Canaan. They were not born hybrid.

First, you have Mizraim, or Egypt. The rulers of the Egyptian people believed that they were descended from the gods. Today, we laugh this off as just human superstition, yet as biblical Christians, we believe God can manifest as a human child with no father.

Chapter 8: The Biblical Origin of Demons

Some have said that the Egyptians existed before the flood. We can very quickly dismantle this idea with the genealogy of Ham's children. Mizraim is Egypt. Mizraim was born around the same time as Nimrod, and therefore, was born after the flood.

Let me show you the biblical evidence that the Egyptian people produced hybrids.

> Egypt was the father of the Ludites, Anamites, Lehabites, Naphtuhites, Pathrusites, Kasluhites (from whom the Philistines came) and Caphtorites. (Genesis 10:13, NIV)

Goliath was a giant hybrid, and he was descended from the line of Mizraim, a son of Anak (Anakim), a descendant of the Caphtorites. Moses took special effort to point out that some of the descendants of the Philistines were of the line of Egypt. This gives us evidence that the hybridization of humans was happening in the days of Nimrod.

Nimrod was a son of Cush and was a mighty man. That word used for "mighty man" is again, *gibbor*. It is the same word used to describe the children of the Sons of the Gods in Genesis 6:4 when Moses says:

> The Nephilim were on the earth in those days, and also afterward, when the sons of God came into the daughters of men, and they bore children to them. Those were the mighty men who were of old, men of renown.

Since we know that the Philistines had giants in their line, and they are descendants of Egypt (Mizraim), we can look at the oldest mummies of the Egyptians and get a sense of what their earliest ancestors may have looked like. The oldest mummies discovered didn't appear to be hybrid. They were very normal.

The word/name Mazor Mizraim is plural. *Mizra* is the root word of the Hebraic word *mazor*, meaning to bind or bandage. I believe this is a prophetic name for the nation because they bandaged or bound their dead in linen wraps.

The Mark of the Beast

One thing that is shown as a similar trait among the Egyptians is that many of their depictions of the gods and the pharaohs have long heads or are wearing hats that make it look like their heads are elongated. The reason they did this was because it was representative or in homage to the original progenitors of Egypt. If you were to google, "Earliest Egyptian mummies," dig around a little, and look at pictures of the oldest mummies found, you would see that they had two traits: red hair and elongated skulls. Some of these Egyptian mummies are housed in the British Museum in England.

As far as elongated skulls go, you can look at the hieroglyphs of the ancient Egyptians and note Pharaoh Khufu's statues and burial mask (his mummy somehow disappeared). He is noted as having an extremely elongated head.

The reason I made mention of this is because of Ham's son, Phut, whose descendants are not mentioned in the Bible. I have speculated that Phut and Mizraim may have been twins because Mizraim is plural in the Hebraic language. This indicates that there were more than one. None of the other children were given plural names. At the very least, they must have shared some similarities.

The Egyptians refer to Punthites (variant of Phutites) in some of their ancient annuls, and many believe that they lived in the area now known as Somalia. However, Josephus and Pliny the Elder both place Phut as being in the land of Libya and west. Now we're about to get a little crazy (as if this whole thing hasn't been crazy enough!)

I would like to refer you back to Genesis 14:5-7. This passage of Scripture discusses the first mention of the Rephaim. The word "Rephaim" (repaim) is derived from the root word *rapha*. We commonly know this word to mean "heal," and it is associated with God's name, Jehovah Rapha. However, when used to describe a race of hybrids, it means a giant, shades/ghosts, or forsaken (no redemption).

Again, you see the same word used to describe the inhabitants in the land of the dead in Proverbs 2:18:

Chapter 8: The Biblical Origin of Demons

> For her house sinks down to death and her ways to the land of the departed spirits. (CSB)

The word used for departed spirits is—you guessed it—Rephaim (repaim).

Let's look at some verses from Isaiah 14:9:

> Sheol from beneath is excited over you to meet you when you come; It arouses for you the spirits of the dead, all the leaders of the earth; It raises all the kings of the nations from their thrones. (NASB 1995)

If you were to read this verse in Hebrew, it would say:

> Sheol below quivers for you. They come against you at your arrival. It stirs up all the Rephaim; all the chiefs stand up from their thrones on the earth, all the kings of the nations and they all testify to you saying, "You have become weak just like we are!"

There's something that you may want to consider for a moment: The spirits of the Rephaim, what we call demons today, are completely aware that they are weak. Colossians 2:15 tells us that Jesus completely defeated those very rulers—the deceased spirits of the Rephaim—that in Isaiah 14 admitted they were weak.

Philippians 4:13 says, "I can do all things through Christ who strengthens me." The Enemy is weak, stripped of power, disarmed, and completely defeated; while we, the disciples of Christ, are strong, equipped, empowered, and completely victorious in Christ Jesus!

Isaiah 14 is the first mention of the Ephesians 6:12 spiritual hierarchy:

> For we wrestle not against flesh and blood, but against principalities, against powers, against the rulers of the darkness of this world, against spiritual wickedness in high *places*.

The Mark of the Beast

The word used for "ruler" in Greek is *arche*, meaning ruler, chief, magistrate, or king. Paul elaborates on the rest of the spiritual forces and their hierarchy, giving us a clearer understanding of what we are dealing with in the spirit realm.

That is enough Scripture to show that the Rephaim are the spirits of the dead. Now I will show you some different scriptures to drive home the point that these spirits are demons.

When I was a young Christian, I believed that all the gods that existed and were worshipped in the ancient days were fallen angels. I mean, logically, the description of certain types of angels describes the appearance of these gods, but that wasn't enough for me. I started to notice that the Bible differentiated between fallen angels and gods very specifically. I learned that the word used to describe God in creation was *Elohim,* which is the plural word for God. Thus, I concluded that this was a revelation of the Trinity.

However, this same word could be used to mean "the gods," as in "the idols," or even human beings. We have several examples of this in the Psalms. For example, Psalm 82:1:

> A Psalm of Asaph. God presides in the divine assembly;
> He renders judgment among the gods. (NIV)

This says in Hebrew:

> God takes His stand in the middle of the congregation of gods; He judges the gods (elohim).

We know from John 10:34-36 that the *elohim* that God was judging in this passage were not angels, but human beings. Jesus answered them:

> Is it not written in your law, I said, Ye are gods? If he called them gods, unto whom the word of God came, and the scripture cannot be broken; Say ye of him, whom the Father hath sanctified, and sent into the world, Thou blasphemest; because I said, I am the Son of God?

Chapter 8: The Biblical Origin of Demons

In this next example, we see the word *el* used to refer to the demons. Exodus 15:11 says:

> Who among the gods (*ba-elim*) is like you, *Yehova*? Who is like you, glorious in holiness, fearful in praises, doing wonders? (emphasis added)

Another scripture in which you see these demons mentioned as *el* is Psalm 77:13. This verse translates as:

> *Elohim* (a reference to the Trinity), Holy is your way. What god (*el*) is so great as our holy God (*Elohim*)?

Upon discovering this revelation, it was highlighted to me by the Holy Spirit that the spirit that is reported to have entered Saul was allowed to come on Saul by God departing; but a few verses later, Samuel notes that the spirit that came on Saul to torment him was from *elohim*.

> After the Spirit of the LORD had departed from Saul, a spirit of distress from the LORD began to torment him. (1 Samuel 16:14, BSB)

This scripture confused me so much. I thought it showed that God could have an evil spirit. That was not the case. This spirit was sent by Yehovah as a sign.

The word translated as "from God" in this verse is *me'et*. This word is tricky. *Ma* is a prefix in Hebrew that means what, why, whereof, or how? *Et* is the Hebrew word *owth*, which means a sign, marker, signal, beacon, omen, or evidence. Reading the passage with this revelation shows that the demon was sent as a sign of God's Spirit turning from Saul. If the Spirit of God is not with you (turned), then the spirit of the Enemy can come upon you.

Allow me to elaborate my last assertion. In Hebrew, it doesn't say the Spirit of the LORD departed from Saul. It says the Spirit of the LORD *sarah* or "turned" from Saul. Whenever it says in the Bible, the

The Mark of the Beast

Spirit of the LORD departed, it says it "turned from." That is also true with the Greek explanation as well.

We know that this spirit was allowed to come upon Saul, and then in verse 23, we see that Samuel notes the spirit was a *ra'ah ruach* (evil spirit) of the gods.

> And so it was, whenever the spirit from God was upon Saul, that David would take a harp and play *it* with his hand. Then Saul would become refreshed and well, and the distressing spirit would depart from him. (1 Samuel 16:23, NKJV)

We commonly think of the word *elohim* as only meaning God, but with this revelation that you now have, you see that the gods (*elohim*) can mean evil gods or idols as well.

> And the evil spirit from the LORD was upon Saul, as he sat in his house with his javelin in his hand: and David played with *his* hand. (1 Samuel 19:9)

When we look at this verse in Hebrew, it says, "And came the spirit from Yahweh distressing Saul." It doesn't say the distressing spirit came from Yahweh. What was going on in this verse was the demon that had come on Saul, when he was being tormented in 1 Samuel 16, came and went from Saul.

The literal words used in Hebrew are *vattehi ruach yehovah ra'ah* (and the spirit from God came distressing *el shaul* (upon Saul).

David played the harp, which ushered in the Spirit of Yehovah, and Yehovah's Spirit distressed Saul, so he tried to kill David, as a result. Demons do not like to be in the presence of God's manifest Spirit, and Saul was clearly demonized after the Spirit of God turned from him in his disobedience, which allowed an evil spirit to come upon him. That spirit was distressed when David ushered in the *Ruach Yahweh* (Spirit of Yahweh) with his music.

This evil spirit of the gods that came on Saul was a spirit of a departed Rephaim. In my opinion, I believe that this demon may have been the

Chapter 8: The Biblical Origin of Demons

spirit of Goliath that David had slain. It was angry that David had killed him, and it wanted vengeance. This is my own conjecture, not a fact or something to create a doctrine over.

In Psalm 96:5, we read, "For all the gods of the nations are idols, but the LORD made the heavens." The word used for "idols" in this scripture is *el-lim,* and the word for "gods" is singular in this case, *elohe*. The Bible very clearly defines that the gods of this world are idols. A side note: this same word can also mean worthless, good for nothing, coming to nothing, or of no value.

You may be wondering how this correlates to the spirits of dead Rephaim being the demons that we know today. Let's explore that topic, shall we? The word for "idols" is not only *elim* in Hebrew. There is another word for idol that is commonly overlooked when we don't research the original Hebrew words that were used in Scripture.

There is a reason that those words were used and placed there. It was for our benefit so that we are left without excuse on the day of judgment.

> For since the creation of the world His invisible attributes are clearly seen, being understood by the things that are made, even His eternal power and Godhead, so that they are without excuse. (Romans 1:20, NKJV)

One of the alternative and earliest words for "idol" in Hebrew is found in Genesis 31:19:

> And Laban went to shear his sheep: and Rachel had stolen the images that *were* her father's.

The word used for "idols" in this verse is *teraphim* (*t-rapim*). The 't' is a silent letter in this word, so it is pronounced *rapim* (Rephaim). The gods that Laban and Rachel worshipped were Rephaim—the spirits of the dead hybrids that were almost completely annihilated in the days of Abraham. It is interesting to notice that we see this word used several times to represent idols, but one in particular that stands out to me is that King David's wife worshipped idols. That was Saul's daughter, Michal.

The Mark of the Beast

> And Michal took an image, and laid it in the bed, and put a pillow of goats' hair for his bolster, and covered it with a cloth. (1 Samuel 19:13)

We see this word used again in Zechariah 10:2, except this time the spirits of *rapim* are personified.

> For the idols (*teraphim/trapim*) speak delusion; the diviners envision lies and tell false dreams; They comfort in vain. Therefore, the people wend their way like sheep; They are in trouble because there is no shepherd.

These idols speak.

Since we now know that the spirits of the Rephaim are demons, we can now understand who or what is speaking through a person when they are demonized. For instance, Jesus was confronted by a legion of demons, which Mark 5:2 describes as an unclean spirit. When they saw Jesus, they cried out and spoke through the man in whom they were staying. You may be thinking, but there's Scripture that says that idols are mute and can't hear (Psalm 115:5, 1 Corinthians 12:2). You are correct, in a sense, but the type of idols they are talking about are wood and stone idols. They are not referring to the spirits that do cause the idols to speak.

I remember listening to the late Reinhard Bonke telling a story of when he was in some foreign country. He asked a priest at the temple of one of their gods something about how the stones are powerless. The priest responded, "The stones are powerless until the spirit of the god enters into it; then the stone comes to life."

Here we have all the evidence that demons are not fallen angels. Even though it says that Satan took one third of the stars with him, that doesn't mean these were angels. In Amos and Acts, the demons Molech and *Rephain* (*Rephan*) (sure looks like Rephaim, doesn't it?) are named and associated with stars. "Stars" is a word that is used in the Old Testament and the New Testament interchangeably to represent Jesus, demons, the people of Israel, and even angels. It's a far stretch

Chapter 8: The Biblical Origin of Demons

to assume that those stars he took with him were angels, since it says the fallen angels are already chained in gloomy darkness. However, the Rephaim have not been judged yet, as we established from the account of the demon-possessed man that met Jesus on the shore of Gadarenes. They said, "Have you come to torment us before the time?"

I want to wrap this up by giving you hope and empowering and equipping you for the total victory that we have been given through Jesus. You have power over demons as a Christian. Demons are just dead, hybrid, half-breed human and animal DNA-tainted spirits of the giants that were defeated by men throughout the Old Testament before the cross. How much greater a victory must you have over them now that they were defeated utterly by Jesus?

I like this little passage in Jeremiah 10:5 that reads:

> Like a scarecrow in a cucumber field, their idols cannot speak; they must be carried because they cannot walk. Do not fear them; they can do no harm, nor can they do any good. (NIV)

Jeremiah paints a picture telling us we have no reason to be afraid of demons. They can't move on their own. They need you to carry them and take them places. What Jeremiah is referencing here is that the actual statues themselves can't walk because they are inanimate objects, but by the same token, I believe that on a deeper level, this is showing that demons only have the ability to impact your life through the actions of others or through your own actions. This is probably why they call witchcraft a work of the flesh and not a work of the spirit.

Therefore, Paul teaches us that we need to control our thoughts and not act in a manner that corresponds to what demons lead people to do. This is why Paul tells us about the works of the flesh:

> Now the works of the flesh are manifest, which are these; Adultery, fornication, uncleanness, lasciviousness, Idolatry, witchcraft, hatred, variance, emulations, wrath, strife, seditions, heresies, envyings, murders,

The Mark of the Beast

drunkenness, revellings, and such like: of the which I tell you before, as I have also told you in time past, that they which do such things shall not inherit the kingdom of God. (Galatians 5:19-21)

The demons that are the manipulating forces behind these acts are trying to get a person to act out these works because it is what they did in their past lives.

Do not yield to these demons anymore. They are defeated. All they want is to try to disqualify you from receiving blessings from God. If they can keep you returning to some kind of blatant sin, they can prevent you from receiving. Paul teaches us:

But the natural man receiveth not the things of the Spirit of God: for they are foolishness unto him: neither can he know them, because they are spiritually discerned. (1 Corinthians 2:14)

These demons were defeated before Jesus came, and they are now utterly defeated because of the finished work of the cross. Come out of agreement with these demons and into agreement with Jesus. You are so much more powerful than demons. They can't even operate without you or someone else allowing them to. They may try to get you to think they can by telling you things like: you have cancer, or you are sick, or something asinine like that, which doesn't line up with the Word of God, because it gives them liberty to attack you.

Come out of agreement with them and into an agreement with God, and then you will have rendered them completely powerless. The BLOOD of JESUS has defeated them! They are hopeless! You are full of the living hope of Christ who lives within you!

Chapter 9: How Are Dead Spirits Still on the Earth?

I'm sure that all of this has been very heavy up to this point. Well, I'd like to tell you it's going to get easier, but I'm not really that kind of teacher.

I have probably attacked some of the doctrines that you learned in church. I would be willing to venture that I offended a stronghold or two, but that's what happens when you start slaughtering sacred cows.

Most of all, I am hoping that I have sparked some questions in your mind and sent you into the Word of God and the internet to see if what I am saying is true. Please don't accept what I am saying as fact or fiction without researching it yourself and testing it to see if I'm right or wrong. You need to discern this for yourself. I am willing to teach and share what has been revealed to me, but you must test it for yourself. No one is perfect.

Now that we have uncovered that demons are the disembodied spirits of the Rephaim hybrids, we need to discuss how this is possible. Many people, including myself, couldn't understand how this was possible because the Bible seems to paint a very clear picture that anyone that dies immediately goes to hell or heaven—or does it? This is a true statement. However, Rephaim hybrids are not pure humans and have a separate designation for punishment.

The Mark of the Beast

While researching this topic, I came upon an interesting revelation from God. Not once is it mentioned that the spirit of a dead, wicked, but genetically pure and untainted human is brought up by a spiritist. When they call up a spirit, it is usually the spirit of a demon that is disguised as a human, but it is never the actual spirit of the human. You may wonder about Samuel in 1 Samuel 28? I considered that myself. Samuel is not dead, and he was not wicked. God is not the God of the dead. Jesus said it this way:

> He is not the God of the dead, but of the living. You are badly mistaken! (Mark 12:27, NIV)

> I am the God of Abraham, the God of Isaac, and the God of Jacob. He is not the God of the dead, but of the living. (Matthew 22:32, NIV)

Well, how can this be? If He is not the God of the dead, then how can He reference these dead people? Simple, you are not dead when you go to heaven. It is commonly taught in the church that, before Jesus, everyone just went to hell and were under the power of the demons, being tormented. That's not the case. We think of verses such as Hebrews 9:27 and Psalm 89:48:

> And as it is appointed unto men once to die, but after this the judgment. (Hebrews 9:27)

> What man can live and never see death? Who can deliver his soul from the power of Sheol? Selah. (Psalm 89:48)

And we say, "See, all men die, and no man can escape from hell."

What it literally says is that everyone must die, and everyone must face judgment. I also see where it says no one can deliver themselves from *Sheol*. Something to remember is that *Sheol* doesn't exclusively mean hell; it also means the grave. To go down to *Sheol* does not mean going to hell every time the word *sheol* is used. It often means they were buried in a grave.

Chapter 9: How Are Dead Spirits Still on the Earth?

Today we would say, who can deliver himself from the grave? To us, that's an obvious answer. God delivers you from the grave; you don't deliver yourself. Hannah says in 1 Samuel 2:6:

> The LORD brings death and gives life; He brings down
> to the grave and raises up. (NKJV)

The only time in the Bible where people are raised up and spoken to after they die were people who are pure human and not genetic hybrids. The instances that we see an interaction between the living and those that passed away are: Saul and Samuel; and Elijah, Moses, and Jesus. All of those men were righteous before God. Elijah himself wasn't even dead; he was taken up to heaven alive, as were Enoch and Jesus. They still must come back and die (barring Jesus who already died once and was resurrected); and then, on top of that, some of the people who are already in heaven will come back with Jesus and rule and reign with Him for 1,000 years, but that's a story for another time. This is possible because, when your body dies and you go to heaven, *you* are not dead.

In the days of old, and even today, a spiritist would conjure familiar spirits. These spirits are spirits that have been assigned to attack certain families. They know everything about the people, and they try to imitate them, imitate their voice, and imitate their spirit, but they are not actually communicating to their dead family members. It's a ruse of the devil.

We see in the story of Lazarus and the rich man that Lazarus died and went to Abraham's bosom in paradise. The rich man appears to have died and gone to hell. The story tells us:

> There was a certain rich man, which was clothed in purple and fine linen, and fared sumptuously every day: and there was a certain beggar named Lazarus, which was laid at his gate, full of sores, and desiring to be fed with the crumbs which fell from the rich man's table: moreover the dogs came and licked his sores. And it came to pass, that the beggar died, and was carried by the angels

The Mark of the Beast

into Abraham's bosom: the rich man also died, and was buried; and in hell he lift up his eyes, being in torments, and seeth Abraham afar off, and Lazarus in his bosom. (Luke 16:19-23)

This story lets us know that the rich man was not righteous. When Lazarus was brought before him, he left Lazarus longing for food to eat and gave him none. Yet, it says that the rich man ate lavishly, and the dogs licked Lazarus's wounds. How humiliating that must have been. Two things happened here: First, Lazarus was not considered cursed or wicked, sinful, or evil when he died. The whole theory that sickness is the result of sin is shot out the window right there. Second, the man that was in hell was a pure human and not a hybrid. This leads us to the conclusion that evil human beings go to hell immediately upon death.

Now that Jesus has come, He set in motion a command stating that no one will get to heaven except through Him. Jesus is the only Way. Before this, the Old Testament, and even Jesus Himself, tell us that some Jews did make it to heaven. I mean, Moses knew God face-to-face, saw even just a fraction of His glory pass before him while he was tucked in a crack on a mountain, and was called the humblest man in all the earth. Abraham greeted Lazarus at the gates of heaven; and yet, some think they died and went to hell. How did Abraham get to heaven before Jesus died? God brought him up.

There is no verse in the Bible that says any part of hell is not a place of torment, yet we have doctrines made up saying Abraham's bosom is a place in hell that acted as a holding tank before Jesus's death and resurrection. Jesse Duplantis tells the story of how he went to heaven, and he met a big barrel-chested man that turned out to be Abraham. Abraham said, "I meet everyone that comes; this is still my bosom."

Now that we have established that pure humans go directly to hell or heaven, we have set the ground for explaining why the Rephaim haven't gone to hell yet. The Bible tells us that the demons go in and out of hell. Let's look at Isaiah 14:9 (BSB) again:

Chapter 9: How Are Dead Spirits Still on the Earth?

> Sheol beneath is eager to meet you upon your arrival. It stirs the spirits of the dead to greet you (Rephaim)— all the rulers of the earth. It makes all the kings of the nations rise from their thrones. (emphasis added)

This is letting us know that hybrid spirits are sitting enthroned on the earth right now, and they go to and from hell when they desire.

The word used to describe the spirits of the dead in Hebrew is Rephaim. They left their throne to meet Satan. You see an Old Testament example of this in Daniel:

> But the prince of the kingdom of Persia withstood me twenty-one days; and behold, Michael, one of the chief princes, came to help me, for I had been left alone there with the kings of Persia. (Daniel 10:13, NKJV)

Paul also makes mention of these rulers in Ephesians 6:12:

> For our struggle is not against flesh and blood, but against the rulers, against the authorities, against the powers of this world's darkness, and against the spiritual forces of evil in the heavenly realms. (NIV)

Ezekiel 32:21 is a prime example of this. In the depths of *Sheol*, the mighty ones (*gibborim eloi*; mighty gods; the same name used in Genesis 6 and Genesis 10) gather in hell and speak to the people that were just slain. In this sense, they are mocking the fallen humans. The word used for mighty in this scripture is *gibborim*. *Eloi* is the word used for gods, and it is referring to idols. Put these two words together and we see "mighty gods."

The Nephilim discussed in Ezekiel 32 are not fallen angels. When you read this chapter in context, you see that the Nephilim in this case are the humans that fell in combat. Remember, angels can't die. Therefore, they are not able to fall to the sword and die and go to hell.

The Mark of the Beast

It's commonly taken for granted that since Jesus now holds the keys to hell and the grave, this insinuates that the gates of hell were closed when Jesus rose from the grave and defeated hell completely. While it is true that Jesus holds the keys to death and the grave, or as Revelation 1:18 states, death and Hades, the context in which it is used appears to imply His total victory over hell and the grave, and that those keys are responsible for life, death, and resurrection to some extent.

My friend Bryan Melvin was judged in heaven when he died as an atheist, and he saw that Jesus had a huge key chain with many different keys on it. Bryan knew in an instant that He did hold the keys to death and the grave.

Jesus specifically told Peter that the gates of hell will not prevail against the church. The word used in this particular scripture is *pule*; a large door; an entrance gate to a city or fortress, which refers to the exit people use to go out, focusing on what proceeds out of it. In Jesus's time, gates represented power and great strength and safety. The larger and stronger the gate was, the more difficult it was for anyone to overtake the gate. Jesus gave Peter, and subsequently us, the power to bind and loose in the heavens and on earth.

In today's modern Christian vernacular, we understand binding and loosing as speaking something out, either positive or negative. I believe Jesus was informing Peter to be mindful of his words and use them to prevent hell from overcoming his life. It would also seem that Peter was being informed in a subtle manner that he was not going to go to hell because Jesus was going to have total victory over the grave, and He secretly knew that Peter would gladly surrender his life to Him as Lord, Messiah, Savior, and Redeemer. However, Jesus also knew that Peter would deny Him before men, and He specifically said that anyone who denies Him before men, the Father would deny. Jesus knew that Peter was going to deny Him three times. He knew that Peter was going to recall that and feel ashamed and guilty. I would dare to speculate that Peter thought that since he rejected Jesus, Jesus would in turn reject him. I bet that's why Jesus made Peter admit that he loved him three times. He had to profess it. He had to use his words as the keys to death

Chapter 9: How Are Dead Spirits Still on the Earth?

and the grave and open the door that bound him in shame and condemnation so he could walk in the resurrected power of Christ.

Hybrid beings are not the creation of God. However, one could say they are a result of His words, since all things are created through God's Word. At some point, Jesus, God, and the Holy Spirit must have spoken about how demons would come to be.

Demons are a twisting of God's Word. They are a deviation of God's original design into something that hardly resembles a man in a spiritual, and in many cases, a physical sense. Based on Genesis 3:15, I believe that the Rephaim that appeared after the flood were the serpent's own bloodline because it says, "And I will put enmity between you and the woman, and between your seed and her Seed; He shall bruise your head, and you shall bruise His heel." The word "seed" in this context is speaking of the children produced from coitus.

Don't get me wrong; I am not saying that Satan created the hybrids. But I am saying that he corrupted the flesh of men by manipulating the serpent to mingle his seed with the seed of mankind. Satan cannot create; he can only corrupt and twist what is already present. Technically, since everything exists due to Jesus speaking it, then what we see corrupted and polluted is a twisting of God's Word. This is what Satan has been doing from day one. He twists God's Word and produces hybrids like dinosaurs, Rephaim, etc.

What is interesting is that Satan seems to believe that it is better to be flesh than it is to be a pure spirit. Everything he does appeals to the flesh.

There is something about human beings that is significantly unique compared to angels. The reason the hybrid Rephaim are not in hell being tormented yet is that it is not yet the appointed time.

Near the tombs at Gadarenes, when the legion of demons came and threw themselves before Jesus, begging Him not to cast them out, they said, "What do you want with us, Son of God? Have you come here to torture us before the appointed time?" The word used for "time" in this verse is *kairos*. This means the exact perfect time when it is the most beneficial.

The Mark of the Beast

The reason God has not forced these demons into the lake of fire (their final place of torment after the day of judgment) is that it isn't the right time yet. The scripture to support this comes from the very mouth of Jesus Christ, our Lord and our Savior:

> The kingdom of heaven is like a man who sowed good seed in his field; but while men slept, his enemy came and sowed tares among the wheat and went his way. But when the grain had sprouted and produced a crop, then the tares also appeared. So the servants of the owner came and said to him, 'Sir, did you not sow good seed in your field? How then does it have tares?' He said to them, 'An enemy has done this.' The servants said to him, 'Do you want us then to go and gather them up?' But he said, 'No, lest while you gather up the tares you also uproot the wheat with them. Let both grow together until the harvest, and at the time of harvest I will say to the reapers, "First gather together the tares and bind them in bundles to burn them but gather the wheat into my barn." (Matthew 13:24-30, NKJV)

Jesus then goes into detail explaining what this parable means to his disciples in private, saying:

> He who sows the good seed is the Son of Man (Jesus, the Seed of the woman). The field is the world, the good seeds are the sons of the kingdom, but the tares are the sons of the wicked one (seed of the serpent). The enemy who sowed them is the devil, the harvest is the end of the age (the day of judgment), and the reapers are the angels. Therefore as the tares are gathered and burned in the fire, so it will be at the end of this age. The Son of Man will send out His angels, and they will gather out of His kingdom all things that offend, and those who practice lawlessness, and will cast them into the furnace of fire. There will be wailing and gnashing of teeth. Then

Chapter 9: How Are Dead Spirits Still on the Earth?

> the righteous will shine forth as the sun in the kingdom of their Father. He who has ears to hear, let him hear! (Matthew 13:37-43, NKJV) (emphasis added)

The simple answer as to why God allows the Rephaim spirits to remain and lead the nations astray is because if He uproots all the evil now, He will not be able to get the benefit of the full harvest of souls. Jesus wants to save every soul that can be saved and will be saved before the day of judgment. He includes the human sinners in this category as well. Not everyone that will come to Christ has come to Him yet. It is hard for us to understand why humans are so important to Him, yet we are. If He knew that He could save every single soul by waiting 10,000 years for everyone to turn to Him, then He would. We are the most important thing to Jesus. We are the hope that was set before Him that strengthened Him to endure the cross.

> Looking unto Jesus, the author and finisher of *our* faith, who for the joy that was set before Him endured the cross, despising the shame, and has sat down at the right hand of the throne of God. (Hebrews 12:2, NKJV)

Chapter 10: The Substance of Nightmares

Everyone knows the scripture where Jesus says that the end times will be like the days of Noah. If not, let me refresh your memory.

> Just as it was in the days of Noah, so also will it be in the days of the Son of Man. (Luke 17:26, NIV)

At the time that Jesus said this, He was telling His disciples what it would be like on the day of His return. Everyone will be living their lives, and all of the sudden, Jesus will come back like a flood. But why did Jesus specify that it would be like it was in the days of Noah?

The word used in Luke 17 that we translate, "as it was" doesn't mean that at all. I am not sure how that came to be the translation. The Greek word used here is *egeneto*. This word is derived from the word *ginomai*. This is an interesting word to be used here. *Ginomai* literally means to become, to come to pass, to transition, to come into being, to manifest, movement, or growth, or to be born. *Egeneto* is derived from *gen*, which is where we get the word genes (genos in Greek) and genesis.

Jesus, in a very subtle manner, likens the events that occur at the end of days with birth pains:

The Mark of the Beast

> Nation will rise against nation and kingdom against kingdom. There will be famines and earthquakes in various places. All these are the beginning of birth pains. (Matthew 24:7-8, NIV)

This is one of those subtle, hidden nuances that Jesus puts in front of our face, yet we cannot see it until He gives us the revelation.

Given this information, we can gain an understanding of what will happen in the last days. If the world is going to be like it was in the days of Noah, then we can expect to see something happen. I believe that "something" is going to be the re-emergence of hybrids and advanced technology on the face of the earth.

The one thing that Moses specifically pointed out to us in Genesis—in the days of Noah—was that the earth was populated with the seed of hybrid human-beast creatures. If Jesus said that it will be like those days, then it's safe to conclude that this is what will be happening again. This is the sign that He gave us by using the word *ginomai,* and His declaration of birthing pains in the end days.

The reason I say that there will be advanced technology is because of what was going on in the days of Nimrod. He was a wicked man. He was married to his mother, he was defiant of God, he wanted to unite man under his rule, and he wanted to recreate man in his own image. These are all telltale signs of the antichrist spirit at work.

In Nimrod's time, there were great advances in technology. Some would cite the book of Enoch, which shares that the fallen Nephilim angels were sharing advanced secrets of science, math, and astrology. The Egyptians, or Mizraim, were making pyramids out of white bricks and bitumen as described in Genesis chapter 11. Tribes of natives and diverse cultures around the world have stories of "star gods" coming from the sky and sharing their technology, and in in some cases, even transforming humans into "gods."

The Mesopotamian hieroglyphs depict electricity. Egyptian hieroglyphs depict spaceships, tanks, helicopters, lightbulbs, etc. And the

Chapter 10: The Substance of Nightmares

ancient Indian Vimana depicts aircraft, spacecraft, mercury motors, advanced surgeries, nuclear weapons, and more.

I remind you of all this to refresh your memory for what we are about to discover next. Much of this may be very new or controversial to what you have been taught previously. Although, I'm fairly certain that much of this has contradicted what you've been taught or previously guessed about this topic.

We're about to jump around in the book of Daniel a little bit, but before we do, I would like to point out a certain word that is often used in the Bible: *gibbor*.

We see this word used four times in Genesis in correlation to the hybrids, then we do not see it again until Deuteronomy 10:17 when it is referring to God as being mighty.

> For the LORD your God is God of gods and Lord of
> lords, the great God, mighty and awesome, who shows
> no partiality and accepts no bribes.

The word *gibborim* is hidden and usually lost in the English translation of this verse.

In Hebrew, the verse reads as such:

> For Yahweh your God of the gods, Lord of the lords, the
> God great, mighty, and awesome who shows no regard
> for persons and takes no bribes.

In this sense, we see not only how great and powerful God is, but this verse is designed to inform us of the fact that the God we serve (in this case, Israel serves) is the God above all the gods and Lord above all the lords of the world. This is a direct reference to the rulers in high places of Ephesians 6, the chief rulers in Daniel, the *gibborim eloi* (the mighty gods) of Ezekiel 32, and the mighty chiefs mentioned in Isaiah 14. God is setting up His preeminence over all these demons.

The Mark of the Beast

It's also important to note that not every time the words "mighty men" are used in the Bible do they mean the hybrids. The Bible makes a significant distinction between the Rephaim and the pure humans. The Bible also makes it a point to trace the genealogy of each significant person described as a mighty man that is a human being. Their lineage can be traced back so we can see that none of them were a hybrid offspring from one of the Rephaim tribes.

Often, the title "mighty men" used to describe brave men that led Israel to victory is *gibborim*. In most cases, they are described as mighty men of valor. On another note, this could be indicating that people in Noah's time were warlike. Usually, the *gibborim* mentioned in the Old Testament were warriors.

The *gibborim* from the book of Genesis, however, are the things of nightmares. As I previously discussed, they are the embodied form of what we call demons today. That being said, let's talk about a dream in the Bible that involves such hybrids that you may not have ever been aware of. Let's look at Nebuchadnezzar's dream involving hybrids and more.

Dreams are such interesting enigmas. To some, a dream is nothing more than a way for your brain to process information from the day. To others, dreams are messages about the future and warnings of things to come. Dreams can also be random firings of neurons that have no meaning or purpose.

Today's modern society has been trying to find the purpose of dreams, and yet, the secular world is still only partially unraveling a small part of the relevance of dreams in our lives. When you ask what a dream means, you are opening the door to a world of hidden treasures, many of which can only be answered in the Word of God.

After waking up from a very peculiar dream, I often find myself asking, "What does that mean?" One day, while doing some research on famous people that had stories inspired by dreams, scientific breakthroughs inspired by dreams, music compilations, and more, I discovered that Mary Shelley, the author of *Frankenstein*, wrote her entire story based on a dream that she had while partaking in a friendly competition

Chapter 10: The Substance of Nightmares

among her friends to come up with the most terrifying horror story. When she was recounting the dream, she said (I am paraphrasing here) that she saw a man who was practicing witchcraft or some unholy art kneeling beside something that he had put together resembling a human-like amalgamation and a large engine. When the engine powered up, the body was jolted enough to begin to stir and come to life.

I find it interesting that she noted the person she saw was a student of witchcraft, or as she called it, unhallowed, unholy, and wicked arts. When I read this dream, I was struck by the correlation of her dream that inspired her re-born, undead monster-man, and something that I had read in the Bible a little while ago.

You may be wondering, what does this have to do with the Bible? Here's what. Let's look at Nebuchadnezzar's dream in Daniel 2:

> Your Majesty looked, and there before you stood a large statue—an enormous, dazzling statue, awesome in appearance. The head of the statue was made of pure gold, its chest and arms of silver, its belly and thighs of bronze, its legs of iron, its feet partly of iron and partly of baked clay. While you were watching, a rock was cut out, but not by human hands. It struck the statue on its feet of iron and clay and smashed them. Then the iron, the clay, the bronze, the silver and the gold were all broken to pieces and became like chaff on a threshing floor in the summer. The wind swept them away without leaving a trace. But the rock that struck the statue became a huge mountain and filled the whole earth. (Daniel 2:31-35, NIV)

This dream is an end-time dream. The reason I can say that is because, when I look at it, I see several indicators. As dream interpreters, my wife and I teach that it is important to look for indicators that signify what type of dream a person is having. If you see a front door, a window, the news, or something speaking of things to come, this will show that the dream is prophetic, or a vision.

The Mark of the Beast

Interpreting Nebuchadnezzar's dream, Daniel tells him that he is seeing things to come:

> After you, another kingdom will arise, inferior to yours. Next, a third kingdom, one of bronze, will rule over the whole earth. (Daniel 2:39)

This makes the dream prophetic—of things to come.

Since I am aware that you can correlate any dream symbol to the Bible, I then start to read the original Hebrew or Greek. This is where I found the most interesting thing, and it is why Mary Shelly's dream stood out to me.

When you read the original Hebrew, you see that Daniel mentions a kingdom of bronze, which is the third kingdom that comes after his. The word used for bronze is *nahasha,* which is pronounced *nechash.* This is where I find that our English translation is a little off compared to the Hebrew. *Nechash*, though it was bronze in the dream, is a play on words for witchcraft, snake, divination, witch, sorcery, soothsayer, and so forth. The word *nahasha* means divination. God does things like this throughout the Bible; He uses plays on words to mean something.

We need to stop right here and address something in this scripture. To my surprise, when I was researching the words in Daniel 2:39, I found a couple of words that are not translated correctly at all. This is quite shocking to me. Here's why.

In Akkadian, which is what is being spoken by Daniel in this passage, he uses the word *ara,* which we translate as "inferior," but there is no definition for this word that ever means inferior. This word means earth or land. So, what we have here when it says, "another kingdom inferior to yours shall arise," is saying a kingdom from another earth shall arise.

Another word that is mistranslated is *tequm.* This word means "appointed." So that sentence actually says after you *tequm* appointed

Chapter 10: The Substance of Nightmares

a kingdom (*umalku*). In modern English, this reads: a place after is appointed another kingdom.

Getting back on topic, God uses plays on words for dreams and visions. For example, Jeremiah says, "I see the branch of an almond tree" (Jeremiah 1:11). The Hebrew word for "almond" is *saqed*. Then God responds and says He is "ready to accomplish His Word." The Hebrew word for "ready" is *soqed*. Here God is demonstrating how He uses word plays symbolically to represent something else.

Since you now know that God uses plays on words, we can look back at Nebuchadnezzar's dream and see that God was using a play on *nechash* (bronze) to represent witchcraft or a serpent. The third kingdom that came was a kingdom of witchcraft or a serpent that ruled over the land—a serpent kingdom.

This same serpent kingdom is mentioned in Revelation chapter 12:17. We typically read this portion of scripture as being symbolic of Jesus being born and the devil trying to kill Him. However, verse 17 gives a better understanding of what is going on and what is being described by John the revelator.

> Then the dragon was enraged at the woman and went off to wage war against the rest of her offspring—those who keep God's commands and hold fast their testimony about Jesus. (Revelation 12:17, NIV)

This is not speaking of going after Jesus, because it says those who hold fast to the testimony of Jesus. This is speaking about Christians that hold on to their belief. In Greek, it says: *The dragon was provoked with the woman and went to make war with the rest of the children.*

The word used here for "with" is *meta* in Greek. This word denotes a change or transformation. The word for children is *spermatos*. This is where we derived the word sperm. This word literally means "the seed of woman." The serpent that pursues the woman is the Antichrist that seeks to alter the seed of woman, just as is prophesied in Genesis 3.

The Mark of the Beast

There have been several kingdoms that came and went since the time of Nebuchadnezzar, yet he only identified four in his dream. By and large, most biblical scholars assume that this was the Greek empire, the Roman empire, and a final empire that is yet to come. However, I do not believe that to be the end all be all. This last kingdom we will see later in Daniel is nothing like any of the other kingdoms that existed.

Daniel said that this witchcraft/serpent empire will rule over all the earth. To date, there has not been a kingdom that has ruled over all the earth. Even in Nebuchadnezzar's time, people knew that as large as his empire was, there were still areas he hadn't conquered yet. You can argue they perceived that he ruled all the earth they were aware existed, but God doesn't give a dream and an interpretation not knowing that there is more world that exists beyond the scope of knowledge the Israelites and Babylonians had at the time.

It's asinine to think that when God gives a man an interpretation of a dream, He limits His infinite knowledge to match the current knowledge of humans. He gives us the truth and lets us seek out the fullness of the revelation as we delve into His Word and gain understanding by chewing and consuming the Word of God as our daily meal.

When we look at the verses where Daniel interprets the dream, we see that he uses a few select words that are solely responsible for triggering my correlation between Mary Shelly's dream and Nebuchadnezzar's dream.

The Hebrew translation of Daniel 2:43 reads:

> As you saw iron mixed with ceramic (this type of ceramic is actually a derivative of something that is dirty, unclean, to be swept away or cast away as useless. It is referring to the purity, or lack thereof, of humankind) clay, they will intermingle with the seed of men, but they will not cling (This is a nice way of saying they will create progeny with humans, but they will not marry. They will have babies, but not marry.

Chapter 10: The Substance of Nightmares

> To cling or to cleave/adhere is how we say a man will leave his parents and will cleave unto his wife) just as iron does not cling to clay. (emphasis added)

What made me correlate Mary Shelly's dream to this dream is that the man in her dream was a student of the unhallowed arts and was creating something that seemingly gave life to a previously dead person. This is a counterfeit of Jesus Christ giving life by resurrecting us from the dead. Frankenstein's monster was a collaboration of several dead people that were manipulated in such a manner as to give the many pieces of several people life through artificial means.

I previously discussed how the word *lehem* in Genesis 4 is left untranslated. It means "to them," but alternatively can mean to burn, to wound, or to rankle. You may also remember that rankle is derived from the word *draco,* meaning dragon in Latin. Therefore, when we see that Daniel refers to humans as ceramic clay, we get a better picture of what is being said. This verse is alluding to the fact that what was going on in the days of Noah will be happening again when the final kingdom of the Antichrist comes into being, in that clay is burned in the fire.

While Frankenstein's monster was not specifically ceramic and iron, he was the remnant of several dead humans. For all intents and purposes, he was a ceramic (synthetic) human. Since we learn from Genesis 1 that we are made of clay, then this monster is, in fact, a type of ceramic clay to the effect that he is an artificial creation and not actually a legitimate, naturally derived human being, though he is part human.

There are a few words that I would like to point out that have been overlooked in the overall prophecy of this dream that Nebuchadnezzar had. The first word is used in Daniel 2:40: *keparzela.* This is a combination of words in Hebrew mixed with some Akkadian. *Ke* means the, that, it, or they, for, or when.

The next part of that word is *parzelah*. This word is believed to be the same word as *barzel* in Hebrew. The reason this word is used is that it's the Akkadian word for iron. Not many people know this,

The Mark of the Beast

but the book of Daniel isn't written entirely in Hebrew. When you consider the fact that Daniel was an Israeli who was in exile in a foreign land, that makes perfect sense.

Let's talk about the etymology of the word "iron" that God used in Nebuchadnezzar's dream. As I stated prior, my wife and I are dream interpreters, and we have noticed a few things about this dream that are remarkable.

Number one, God tends to speak in patterns when He gives a dream. In almost every dream, with a little research, you will find that God used a particular symbol multiple times to express the overall meaning of the dream or the important symbol.

In this dream, one such pattern that we noticed was discovered upon researching the etymology of the word *barzel*. In Hebrew, they believe this word originally meant to drill, to penetrate, or to separate, and was derived from the Hebrew word *birza,* which was a hole in a barrel and is the modern Hebraic word for a faucet. Logically, this makes sense because iron was considered the strongest metal at the time and was used to carve and chisel.

Remember, Genesis 4 says that in the time Enosh was born, they began to profane the name of God. The word for "to profane" is chalal, which means to bore or pierce, to wound, to pollute, to defile.

The second pattern of the dream comes into play when we look at the word *pelag* in Daniel 2:41. Perhaps you recognize this word from Genesis 11 and 1 Chronicles, and the man, Peleg. Perhaps you recognize it from earlier in the book. Whatever the case is, this word is used in the dream that Nebuchadnezzar had.

The word *palag* means to divide, to tear apart like a shirt is torn, or to split. This word is in different variations throughout the Old Testament and almost always means to divide. The handful of times it doesn't mean to divide, it refers to "a divide." For instance, in Job 29:6 and Psalm 13, it means a river. A river stands for division for the fact that it divides and carves its way through something.

With some understanding, you can ascertain the idea that at the end of days, there will be some sort of division that is going to

Chapter 10: The Substance of Nightmares

happen. As I said previously, I believe that God divided the continents in Genesis 11 when the people began to build the Tower of Babel. If God were to split the land apart, there would be a tumultuous shaking of the land because the earth would be split apart. We know that every time the plates of the earth move and shift, there is an earthquake.

Jesus, when speaking of the end of days, says, "Nation will rise against nation and kingdom against kingdom. There will be famines and earthquakes in various places." I believe this means there will be a cataclysmic earthquake that will leave the world reeling and divided, similar to what happened when God created the great continental divide in Genesis 11. I will cover this massive earthquake in a later chapter.

In Daniel 2:42, we read:

> As the toes were partly iron and partly clay, so this kingdom will be partly strong and partly brittle. (NIV)

Upon reading this in English, we lose a little bit of what was being said. There are two different words translated as "partly" in this scripture. The first is *uminehen,* which means "from." The next word used for partly is *qesat*. This is an interesting word. It doesn't mean to divide in the sense we think of it. This word is used five times in the Bible; three are in the book of Daniel, and two are in the book of Exodus, to describe the placement of the cherubim on the ark of the covenant. This word represents "from side to side," such as bookends go on each side of a row of books to keep them in place.

This gives us two separate ideas about what will happen at the end of days. Jesus says in Matthew 24:37, "As it was in the days of Noah, so it will be at the coming of the Son of Man." He is comparing the end of days to the beginning of days.

If you were to take a bookend and label that shelf "Pre-flood" (beginning of days), then sandwich all of the world's history in the middle and cap it off with a bookend labeled, "End of days," you would get a decent illustration of what's being spoken of here.

The Mark of the Beast

This lone word in Daniel's interpretation of Nebuchadnezzar's dream is an indicator of what to expect in the last days. It's a prophetic clue that seems to have gone unnoticed by countless generations—one that points us to the introduction of the Rephaim who seek to alter mankind's DNA yet again, as they did in the days of Noah.

Chapter 11: Unraveling the Mystery of the Beast

The dreams and visions in the book of Daniel are of particular interest to me. You can correlate them with other books that speak of the end of days and get a very distinct idea of what will be going on, and they tie right into the book of Revelation.

In chapter 7, we see Daniel get a deeper revelation about the end of days than what was revealed to him and Nebuchadnezzar in chapter 2 through the king's dream. I would be willing to hypothesize that Daniel was probably intrigued by the king's dream and asked God to show him a deeper revelation of the dream and the events that will take place in the time of the last kingdom. I mean, I have asked God for the same thing, and the nature of men hasn't changed very much throughout human history. According to Solomon, there is nothing new under the sun.

In Daniel 2, we saw the second, third, and fourth kingdoms mentioned. In Daniel 7, we see a fourth kingdom mentioned as well. We know from the book of Revelation that this is referring to the final beast at the end of days.

> And the fourth kingdom shall be as strong as iron, inasmuch as iron breaks in pieces and shatters everything; and like iron that crushes, that kingdom will break in pieces and crush all the others. (Daniel 2:40)

The Mark of the Beast

Daniel 2 reads very similarly to Daniel 7:23:

> He gave me this explanation: "The fourth beast is a fourth kingdom that will appear on earth. It will be different from all the other kingdoms and will devour the whole earth, trampling it down and crushing it. (Daniel 7:23, NIV)

When we look at this in the original language in which it was written, we see an interesting word: *tisne*. This word is translated as "to be different," but its definition is "to change or alter." To be different does imply a change, but it's not as direct as the word "change." I find that to be an interesting choice of words because of the tidbit that was discovered in Revelation 12:17, Jude 7, and Romans, that speaks of altered flesh. It can't be a coincidence that when the Antichrist is mentioned, there is typically a mention of the alteration of flesh.

Surely by now, you're thinking, "No, that can't be right, can it?" That's what I thought, and then the Holy Spirit told me to read the next verse in Daniel 7:

> The ten horns are ten kings who will come from this kingdom. After them, another king will arise, different from the earlier ones; he will subdue three kings. (Daniel 7:24)

You've probably guessed by now that I'm going to tell you what it says in Hebrew, right? Well, you're correct!

> And the ten horns; and from this kingdom, these ten kings shall arise, and from them another king who shall be different from the previous ones and three kings he will humble (subdue).

Take note that at no point does God tell Daniel that the four beasts are human. It says they rise from the earth. You may be thinking, "Well, man is made of earth, therefore, it means they rise up from man." You would be mistaken. The word used for earth in Daniel 7:23 is *ara*. In

Chapter 11: Unraveling the Mystery of the Beast

every instance this variant of the word is used in the Bible, it means earth, as in it will rise up on the earth. Each time Daniel has this vision, he describes what he saw as beasts, and when the revelation is given to him, the one delivering the revelation describes them as beasts.

In verse 25, we see the correlation of this beast and the beast in later chapters of Daniel, as well as the beasts in Revelation. Even in the book of Revelation, these beasts are never referred to as men. Let's take a look at Daniel 7:25 (BSB):

> He will speak out against the Most High and oppress the saints of the Most High, intending to change the appointed times and laws; and the saints will be given into his hand for a time, and times, and half a time.

Here's the Hebrew:

> He will decree against the highest of the Most High. He shall speak and persecute of the holy ones of the Most High, and he shall bear in mind to change the times and to change the law, and they shall be given into his hands for a time, two times, and a half a time (Three and a half years).

The word translated "Most High" is *Ilah,* which is derived from the word *alah* in Hebrew. *Alah* means to ascend. The Antichrist is not only speaking against God, but against Christ, the One who ascended (see John 3:13).

In the book of Revelation, John sees the same vision as Daniel in Chapter 7:

> And I stood upon the sand of the sea, and saw a beast rise up out of the sea, having seven heads and ten horns, and upon his horns ten crowns, and upon his heads the name of blasphemy. (Revelation 13:1)

The Mark of the Beast

Later, in Revelation 17:12-13, John gets this revelation about the ten horns:

> And the ten horns which thou sawest are ten kings, which have received no kingdom as yet; but receive power as kings one hour with the beast. These have one mind and shall give their power and strength unto the beast.

From these passages, we get a revelation of the power they give to the Antichrist. In Greek, it says they give him power and authority. This type of power is *dunamis* power. It is an explosive and miraculous type of power. *Dunamis* is where we get our word "dynamite."

The word for "authority" in this scripture is *exousia*. This word means delegated power. It is referring to a type of power that is given from a higher plane, such as heaven, and delegated to a lower plane, the earth realm. We can gather from this that they not only hand over their control of some area of the world, but they hand over everything they have from both the spirit and natural realm. In turn, the Antichrist then uses this power boost to subdue the earlier three kings that were still in power before he came into being.

God reveals through His Word and by His Spirit what will happen at the end. I encourage you to search these things out further and draw near to Him to hear what He would say to you personally. He will reveal things about the last days, and He will also reveal to you how you can be ready when the time comes.

Chapter 12: Daniel's Visions

Let's go back to what is quickly becoming my favorite book in the Bible: Daniel. In Daniel chapter 8, we see Daniel having another vision that directly correlates to his vision in chapter seven. In this vision, Daniel sees two goats. In the first part of the vision, he describes two goats that he saw, and then in verse 5 he says:

> And as I was considering, behold, an he-goat came from the west on the face of the whole earth, and touched not the ground: and the goat had a notable horn between his eyes. (Daniel 8:5)

I simply had to know what this said in Hebrew. At first glance, it does look a little different than it does in English. In English, it says a he-goat, but there is a little bit more added to that in Hebrew. In Hebrew, it says a he-goat (*tsaphir*) and female goats (*hazizim*) came from the west, across all the earth without touching the ground.

First, you are probably trying to rationalize this as nothing more than a dream. However, when the vision is explained to Daniel, it is described as literal with symbolism in it. The reason God does this is to conceal part of a matter and cause us to seek out the full revelation. In this case, you see that this is exactly what Daniel did. He was given the vision from God and then sought Him for revelation on the matter.

The Mark of the Beast

Two things stood out to me in the Hebrew translation of those verses. The first was the word for female goats; this word ha-ziz-im. I couldn't believe my eyes when I first saw that word. That is nearly the same word that was used to describe Rephaim in Genesis chapter 14:5. In that verse, a tribe of Rephaim is called *Ha-zuzim*. This word is derived from the word *ziz*, which means moving things or beasts. That word is spelled *hazizim* and has the same meaning. There are no coincidences in the Bible, or even in life for that matter. Everything happens for a reason. I'd also like to point out that this is a plural word.

The next part of verse 5 that struck me was that Daniel described it as crossing the land without touching the ground. Again, you could say it's just a dream, but I know that this is not the case. First, it was not a dream; it was a look into an open heaven, which was explained to Daniel by Gabriel. This illustrated that this kingdom would be able to fly. These beasts can fly; they will be in the sky.

There is a double meaning to flying in this dream. Most often, flying in dreams represents the ability to overcome a situation. The thing you fly over indicates what it is you are overcoming. That shows me that these zuzim hybrids (the Antichrist) are overcoming the world. To overcome doesn't always mean something positive. It can also mean to overtake, overthrow, or subdue. In this context, it would mean to overtake the entire world.

To counter any doubters that would say this is about events that have already happened, I would point out the following verses which tell us that these goats are referring to the last days and what we commonly refer to as the Antichrist. We see the four kings represented by the four horns later in the book of Revelation as well.

The chapter continues to say:

> The ram which thou sawest having two horns are the kings of Media and Persia. And the rough goat is the king of Grecia: and the great horn that is between his eyes is the first king. Now that being broken, whereas four stood up for it, four kingdoms shall stand up out of the nation, but not in his power. And in the latter time

Chapter 12: Daniel's Visions

of their kingdom, when the transgressors are come to the full, a king of fierce countenance, and understanding dark sentences, shall stand up. And his power shall be mighty, but not by his own power: and he shall destroy wonderfully, and shall prosper, and practise, and shall destroy the mighty and the holy people. (Daniel 8:20-24)

While I was reading the literal translation of this verse, I saw the word Ba'al. Typically, we look at this passage through the lens that this is a human being. However, since we know that this passage is referring to a Rephaim king, what I'm about to share with you will make a lot more sense.

There is a god that is known as Ba'al, or Ba'al Rephaim, or Ba'al Rap'i'nu. The earliest known mention of the god, Ba'al, is about 2,400 BC. This is an important date. This is shortly after the flood, and it is the time in which Nimrod began his shenanigans, the earth was divided, and new languages were created.

The first mention of the name Ba'al is found as far back as the time of the ancient Sumerians. After the death of Nimrod, the Sumerian people deified Nimrod and called him Ba'al or Bel. The people of ancient Greece called Ba'al Mars or Saturn. Indeed, it's not a coincidence that the stars are named after this deity.

Nimrod was the king of the Rephaim. Nimrod is the king of the daemon (demons). He is the Ba'al. I believe that this is the Ba'al that is mentioned by God by name in a somewhat conspicuous manner in Daniel's dream.

The phrase "understanding dark sentences" stands out to me. I used to read that and think it just meant he was evil. With that train of thought, you can easily dismiss this as meaning he is evil and understands evil. However, this same phrase is used in Numbers when God says that Moses spoke plainly with God, and God does not speak in dark sentences to him. This implies that there is nothing hidden. Dark sentences are an allegorical way of speaking in parables or riddles. They are things that seem to not make sense to most people unless they are given a spirit of wisdom to understand what is being said. Jesus spoke

The Mark of the Beast

in parables to the people. These are dark riddles in the sense that the message of the parable is shrouded in mystery unless otherwise revealed by God. This is what is meant when it says that the false prophet will understand riddles.

We also see another interesting phrase that seems to be lost in translation: fierce features. The word translated as fierce features is *panim*. That word is the plural version of the word pane, which means "faces."

This is an important clue as to what the Antichrist will look like. We also see a reference to the Antichrist having multiple heads in Revelation 13:3:

> And I saw one of his heads as it were wounded to death; and his deadly wound was healed: and all the world wondered after the beast.

These scriptures let us know that, without a doubt, the kingdoms that come from the first beast are not purely human. They are beasts. There will be a second emergence of at least one of the tribes of the Rephaim. I would be willing to speculate that many of these creatures that come from the first beast will share many similar characteristics of the seemingly exterminated Rephaim tribes that, as we read, left evidence of their existence around the world.

As everything began in Israel, in the Middle East, and escalated from there, so it shall be once again—just as in the days of Noah when the ark was built. The reason for this is because certain spirits are trapped in their territories and seem to have only territorial power over the earth. We see a sample of this in Daniel 10:13:

> But the prince of the kingdom of Persia withstood me one and twenty days: but, lo, Michael, one of the chief princes, came to help me; and I remained there with the kings of Persia.

The word for Prince here is *sar*, and it means the chief captain, a task master, governor, keeper, lord, or ruler.

Chapter 12: Daniel's Visions

We see this word used multiple times in the Old Testament: Pharoah's cupbearer, the leaders of battalions, and rulers over cities and nations. It is not just denoting a prince or person of royalty, but a person who is in charge of something.

In Ephesians 6:12, we learned that there are different levels of spiritual rulers that we are dealing with. For we wrestle not against flesh and blood, but against principalities, against powers, against the rulers of the darkness of this world, against spiritual wickedness in high *places*.

Principalities in Greek is the word exousia. This denotes delegated power or jurisdiction. The next verse uses the word *kosmokrateros*, which means "ruler of the world." And then, of course, there are *pneumatika ponerias*—evil spirits.

Demons are aware of these territorial boundaries to which they are assigned. They seem terrified in the story of the man with the legion of demons, and they beg to not be cast out of the country. In Mark 5:10, the demons are speaking to Jesus, and it says he besought him much that he would not send them away out of the country.

By all of this we know that the Antichrist is a Rephaim.

Chapter 13: Daniel's Dream

In this chapter of the book, I want to discuss more of Daniel chapters 7 and 8, and how they correlate to the book of Revelation. The first item is Gabriel's response to Daniel about the vision Daniel had. Verse 23 is of particular interest to me.

I want to start by saying that I am aware that many believe that the defilement of the temple was committed by Antiochus IV. To some extent, it was, however, there is no mention of exactly how long he tormented the Jews and defiled their sanctuary. If he was spoken of in Daniel 8, then I would dare say there would be an exact accounting of this defilement that was precisely 2,300 days (about seven years) that the statue stood in the temple.

What we must understand is that Satan has tried to establish an antichrist since the beginning of time. He tried to eliminate all pure and perfect humans as made by God; and he tried to unite the world under one ruler multiple times and use that ruler to destroy the Jews and eventually Christians. Satan is always trying to fulfill prophecy according to his terms and not according to the terms that the prophets set before us in the collection of books we know as the Bible.

Again, many believe Daniel 8 is related to events that have already come to pass. However, I believe I can dispel this belief with one verse:

The Mark of the Beast

> In the latter part of their reign, when rebels have become completely wicked, a fierce-looking king, a master of intrigue, will arise. (Daniel 8:23, NIV)

The word used in this verse for "the latter part" is *ubeaharit*. This word is used to mean the end of days or the end of times.

Gabriel makes a similar mention about these events, saying:

> And the vision of the evenings and mornings which was told is true; therefore seal up the vision, for it refers to many days in the future. (Daniel 8:26, NKJV)

I don't have to translate this into its literal translation because this current text does the job quite well. Gabriel makes a clear reference to the end of a day and the beginning of a day. The Hebraic understanding was that the days began at night and ended at night. However, their workdays didn't begin until the sun came up, in most cases, just as our days (depending on the person) don't start until the sun is up. We consider a new day when the sun rises. Because Gabriel used this very distinct expression, we see that he was indicating the end of the day.

Even though we know that the new day technically begins at 00:00 (12:00 a.m.), we still consider the metaphorical beginning of our day to be when the sun rises (again, that's barring the brave few that work the night shift).

To better illustrate this, I would again refer you to the picture in your mind—a bookend labeled end of the day (sunset), and beginning of the day (sunrise), and the rest of the day in between those two bookends. This represents the beginning and end of the day, or to more clearly say it, the end of days. We don't count evenings and mornings as new days; we count them as the same day. They are simply different ends of the same day.

One could argue that the Hebrews believed the days began at sunset. Yes, that's correct. The emphasis on these words is that they represent sunset to sunrise, dusk till dawn, or day's end to daybreak. In the same

Chapter 13: Daniel's Dream

token, this is a reference to, "As it was at the beginning of the days, so shall it be at the end of the days."

Now that we have established it is referring to end-time prophecy, let's discuss another little tidbit that is generally overlooked. The four rams mentioned at the beginning of the chapter have something in common with both the book of Revelation and chapter 7 of the book of Daniel. In Daniel 7:2, we see that four winds, or spirits, depending on which translation you read, stirred up the sea. In English, it says they strove upon the sea. What is says in Hebrew is that they broke forth the Great Sea and up from it came the four beasts.

It's important to note that the revelation that John was given was not given to him in chronological order. God exists outside of time, and therefore, heaven is outside of the confines of time as well. The evidence of this book not being in chronological order is that he starts by giving a now word to the churches. Then John is called up into heaven.

He starts to describe what he sees in the throne room of God. In chapter 5, he tells of the four horsemen and the coming of the Lord. In the next chapter, God seals the Jews, raptures the church after the tribulation, and up until chapter 11, speaks of what will happen. Then, suddenly, John jumps back to when Jesus was born, even though he had just said a few chapters back that the Lamb that was slain for us was already in heaven. After this, he writes about the beast that rises up out of the sea again. That being said, let's try to piece together what Daniel saw and get a better understanding of what is going on in the book of Revelation.

In Revelation, the four winds were held back and prevented from harming the earth, the sea, or the trees. In the book of Daniel, four beasts rise from the sea, and each one is representative of a kingdom. The reason this stands out to me is that the word for spirit, wind, and breath is the word *ruach* in Hebrew. In Greek, we typically see the word *pneumati* used to describe a spirit, but in the case of Revelation 7:1, we see John refer to the spirits as winds. The Greek word used here is *anemos*. This word is derived from the word *ane,* meaning to breathe, or wind. I can't help but notice the partial similarity between this word and the word ruach in Hebrew.

The Mark of the Beast

From this perspective, it is quite easy to see that the four winds, or spirits, that were being held back are the same spirits in Daniel and Revelation. We see later in Revelation 9 that the four angels are released, and they have a specific number of troops, which is twice 10,000 times 10,000. I'm not sure exactly what that means or if I am correct, but 10,000 times 10,000 is 100,000,000, multiplied by two is 200,000,000 soldiers. It appears that these same soldiers are under the command of the four winds (apparently spirits) and kill one-third of the population, which (if this happened today) would be approximately 2.3 billion people.

Another similarity I see is that the beasts mentioned in Daniel's prophecies and the beasts mentioned in Revelation are never called humans. They are always called beasts. Some scholars conjecture that this signifies they have a beastly nature, meaning they are wild and act like metaphorical animals.

The word used for beast in Greek is *therion*. This word is only ever used to describe wild creatures and dangerous animals every time it is used in the New Testament. In the same sense, the word that Daniel uses to describe the beasts is *chevah*. This variant of the word is used twenty times, only in the book of Daniel, and only means beast or wild animal.

In the case of the beast, though, we know he is not simply three kings. Gabriel is careful to point out that the final beast is a king that rises out of one of the four beast kingdoms on the earth at the end of days. This beast apparently has "faces." This probably seems like poppycock to you at this point, but if you continue reading, you will see how this is possible.

Chapter 14: The Four Beast Kingdoms

Anyone can read Daniel Chapter 7 and get an idea that the four beasts mentioned in Daniel's vision correlate to the beasts that are mentioned in Revelation 13. Daniel 7:3-6 tells us that the four beasts come up individually. He describes them as being like a lion, a bear, a leopard, and the fourth more terrible. Each one of these beasts is described as "da min da," or different from one another.

We see the same description coming from John, except he says that he saw one beast coming from the sea. John specifically used the word *tes* for "the." In most Latin-based languages, the word for "you," or "they," or anything indicating plurality, is typically transformed from *te* or *tu* to *tes* or *les*. In French, they don't say God bless you at the end of a sneeze. They say, "*a tes souhaits*" or "*a tes amis*," or they say "*a tes amours*." This means, "to your wishes," "to your loved ones," and "to your loves." It indicates a blessing upon your loved ones and receiving a blessing in your life.

In ancient Greek, the same principle applies. If something is plural, meaning more than one, rather than saying y'all, as we do down south, it is expressed as *tes* in the Latin/Greek. This is the equivalent of y'all in the south. This notation seems to take away the idea that the beast was one beast and was not four as Daniel had said.

The Mark of the Beast

Another key aspect that is lost in translation is that the word used to describe the beast is plural as well. The word used is *therion*. This word is significant on more levels than just that it was an animal in nature, and it was plural.

This ties in significantly with the clay that is mentioned in Nebuchadnezzar's dream in Daniel 2. The type of clay described as mixing with ceramic clay is *tina*. This word is derived from the root word tit (pronounced teet), which means mud, mire, or clay. This type of mud is like a type of dirt that is to be swept away by a broom. This word is typically used to convey a type of utter defeat wherein the Enemy of God is stomped into the mud as we see in 2 Samuel 22:43:

> Then I beat them as fine as the dust of the earth; I trod them like dirt in the streets, and I spread them out. (2 Samuel 22:43, NKJV)

If you are familiar with working with clay, then you are most likely aware that any impurity or imperfection in the clay will cause the integrity of the clay to be compromised, and the creation of the potter is no longer fit for use. Typically, if you have even so much as an air bubble in a piece of clay when you fire it in the kiln, it will cause the pottery to shatter or break apart in the intense heat.

This is also significant in how it pertains to the end of days being like the days of Noah in the fact that Noah was declared to be perfect in his generations. As stated previously in this book, that word for "perfect" is *tamim*, which means without spot or imperfection, pure, perfect, blameless. This was an indication that his flesh was not corrupted by any DNA that is not human. He was not a hybrid. So, we see again that there will be another mixing of some sort that occurs at the end of days. Knowing this will help you to see how Nebuchadnezzar's dream ties into Daniel's dream of the four beasts.

We see that the four beasts are not just one beast as was thought to be the case upon first reading Revelation 13. They are four distinct beasts that we are told rise from the sea because of four spirits being

Chapter 14: The Four Beast Kingdoms

loosed upon the earth. As a result of this release, several things occur which set the stage for the beasts to come forth.

As I stated previously, Daniel 7:23 gives us an indication that the four kingdoms mentioned are beast kingdoms. The words used to describe these kingdoms are always beasts. It's important to take note that these types of beasts are not the living creatures we see in Revelation; they are literal beasts. The word used to describe the beasts always pertains to something that is unclean and cannot be used at the altar as a sacrifice.

> Therefore, I urge you, brothers and sisters, in view of God's mercy, to offer your bodies as a living sacrifice, holy and pleasing to God—this is your true and proper worship. (Romans 12:1, NIV)

Our bodies, our lives even, are meant to be offered to God as a sacrifice. That means that we are acceptable to be burned at the altar. Don't get me wrong, I don't condone human sacrifice; what I am saying is that the Holy Spirit is the fire: "For our God is a consuming fire." (Hebrews 12:29)

The implication given to us by Daniel and John the revelator is that these beasts are not of God, nor are they for God. Since the beasts are not fit for sacrifice, that means they are not accepted by God. They are not human, we are not descended from them, they are not our saviors, and prophecy about Messiah Jesus is not about these beast kingdoms. Their bodies and their lives are not fit for sacrifice. We can be assured that the lifestyle of these beasts and beast kingdoms is unholy.

As we see in the book of Daniel and in the book of Revelation, the beasts are said to rise out of the sea. I believe those four beast kingdoms are descendants of the serpent from the garden in the book of Genesis. I believe they are his biological children. I know this sounds crazy to you, and when God first showed me, I thought it was crazy too!

Extra biblically, the dead sea scrolls that were discovered contain the book of Enoch and a book referred to as the book of Giants. In these books, you see that the Rephaim were called bastard spirits and that

The Mark of the Beast

there were giant men as well as giant beasts. These texts describe the beasts as having the ability to speak.

There are creatures that are described in the Bible as being sea creatures. In Job 41:1, God describes a sea monster or creature as Leviathan. Many assume this is referring to a giant squid, a shark, an alligator, or something they can fathom in the natural world. It's perfectly natural for a person to want to do that because it means you have to take the Bible as being literal. If the Bible isn't literal, then it's just stories designed to guide us and therefore has no bearing on our lives.

Leviathan is described in Psalm 74:13-15 as well:

> You divided the sea by Your strength; You broke the heads of the sea serpents in the waters. You broke the heads of Leviathan in pieces, and gave him as food to the people inhabiting the wilderness. You broke open the fountain and the flood; You dried up mighty rivers. (NKJV)

We see in verses 13 and 14 that the heads of the serpents and the heads of Leviathan are described as two separate entities. The word used to describe the sea serpents is *tannim*. This is derived from the word *tan*, meaning serpent, or sea serpent; although today, in many Bible versions, it is translated as jackals (which is again another attempt to understand the supernatural by reducing it to something fathomable to the natural mind). Not once is the word used to describe a jackal or a crocodile.

When you think about it, why would Pharoah be afraid of a staff like the one Aaron had in Exodus 7 that turned into a snake? I'm sure the Egyptians were quite accustomed to dealing with snakes in their time. Janes and Jambres could do the same thing.

I can see how someone could deduce that the staff was turned into a crocodile; that's intimidating, but still, as a king, you would just have your guards kill it. Even today, people wrestle and overtake crocodiles with their own strength and skill. God very clearly describes Leviathan to Job: It shoots fire from its mouth, it is huge and strong, it has armor for skin, and so much more. Last time I checked, crocodiles didn't have the ability to breathe fire or have flashes of light come from them. If God

Chapter 14: The Four Beast Kingdoms

was just exaggerating Leviathan, He would be a liar. However, God cannot lie. So, when He describes Leviathan, He is describing the real thing. There is no deceit in Him.

> Can you pull in Leviathan with a fishhook or tie down its tongue with a rope? Can you put a cord through its nose or pierce its jaw with a hook? Will it keep begging you for mercy? Will it speak to you with gentle words? Will it make an agreement with you for you to take it as your slave for life? Can you make a pet of it like a bird or put it on a leash for the young women in your house? Will traders barter for it? Will they divide it up among the merchants? Can you fill its hide with harpoons or its head with fishing spears? If you lay a hand on it, you will remember the struggle and never do it again! Any hope of subduing it is false; the mere sight of it is overpowering. No one is fierce enough to rouse it. Who then is able to stand against me? Who has a claim against me that I must pay? Everything under heaven belongs to me. I will not fail to speak of Leviathan's limbs, its strength, and its graceful form. Who can strip off its outer coat? Who can penetrate its double coat of armor? Who dares open the doors of its mouth, ringed about with fearsome teeth? Its back has rows of shields tightly sealed together; each is so close to the next that no air can pass between. They are joined fast to one another; they cling together and cannot be parted. Its snorting throws out flashes of light; its eyes are like the rays of dawn. Flames stream from its mouth; sparks of fire shoot out. Smoke pours from its nostrils as from a boiling pot over burning reeds. Its breath sets coals ablaze, and flames dart from its mouth. Strength resides in its neck; dismay goes before it. The folds of its flesh are tightly joined; they are firm and immovable. Its chest is hard as rock, hard as a lower millstone. When it rises up, the mighty are terrified; they retreat before its thrashing. The sword that reaches it has no effect, nor

The Mark of the Beast

does the spear or the dart or the javelin. Iron, it treats like straw and bronze like rotten wood. Arrows do not make it flee; slingstones are like chaff to it. A club seems to it but a piece of straw; it laughs at the rattling of the lance. Its undersides are jagged potsherds, leaving a trail in the mud like a threshing sledge. It makes the depths churn like a boiling caldron and stirs up the sea like a pot of ointment. It leaves a glistening wake behind it; one would think the deep had white hair. Nothing on earth is its equal— a creature without fear. It looks down on all that are haughty; it is king over all that are proud. (Job 41:1-34, NIV)

Just a side note here; did you catch that it says Leviathan leaves a trail of its belly prints in the mud? This implies to me that Leviathan does not have any legs. Remember that for later in the book.

Chapter 15: The Four Kingdoms Become One

Here is a terrifying thought: the world is going to undergo a series of changes and divisions as a result of large cataclysmic earthquakes. The faces of the nations, seashores, and borders are going to change because of this great divide. There will be great famines, and a sizable portion of the world will undergo a catastrophe when the angel of Revelation 8:7 blows the trumpet and one-third of the earth is burned with fire. This is the precursor to the great earthquake that buries the mountains under water in Revelation 16.

While researching this topic, I discovered that a large portion of all major earthquakes happen during a massive drought. Several studies have shown that there was a drought that occurred at the same period as the days of Nimrod (approximately 2,400-2,200 BC). There have been assorted studies that show dust records with pollen and various other aspects in remote parts of the world, deep within caves, that have no scientific reason for being where they were found.

This was quite a revelation to me because, for the continents to be split, I believe it is safe to assume there must have been a massive earthquake at that time. There were also probably massive earthquakes at the time of the flood as well. It says that the waters of the deep burst forth out from their underground caverns. Logically, if a chasm appears,

The Mark of the Beast

revealing a deep cavern full of living water, that tells me there was most likely some form of seismic activity.[7]

Let's get back on topic and focus on the title of this chapter, shall we? We know that there will one day be four kingdoms that control the entirety of the world. What I find interesting is that the four kingdoms that are spoken of in the book of Daniel have kings of the North and kings of the South. Meanwhile, we see that the Christians are still here on the earth at that time (at least momentarily).

It would behoove us to read another portion of Scripture from Daniel:

> And both these kings' hearts shall be to do mischief, and they shall speak lies at one table; but it shall not prosper: for yet the end shall be at the time appointed.
>
> Then shall he return into his land with great riches; and his heart shall be against the holy covenant; and he shall do exploits, and return to his own land.
>
> At the time appointed he shall return, and come toward the south; but it shall not be as the former, or as the latter.
>
> For the ships of Chittim shall come against him: therefore he shall be grieved, and return, and have indignation against the holy covenant: so shall he do; he shall even return, and have intelligence with them that forsake the holy covenant.
>
> And arms shall stand on his part, and they shall pollute the sanctuary of strength, and shall take away the daily sacrifice, and they shall place the abomination that maketh desolate.

---

7. Wright, K. (1998, March 1). *Empires in the Dust*. Discover-Magazine. Retrieved January 31, 2023, from https://www.discovermagazine.com/planet-earth/empires-in-the-dust .

Chapter 15: The Four Kingdoms Become One

> And such as do wickedly against the covenant shall he corrupt by flatteries: but the people that do know their God shall be strong and do exploits.
>
> And they that understand among the people shall instruct many: yet they shall fall by the sword, and by flame, by captivity, and by spoil, many days.
>
> Now when they shall fall, they shall be holpen with a little help: but many shall cleave to them with flatteries.
>
> And some of them of understanding shall fall, to try them, and to purge, and to make them white, even to the time of the end: because it is yet for a time appointed.
>
> And the king shall do according to his will; and he shall exalt himself, and magnify himself above every god, and shall speak marvellous things against the God of gods, and shall prosper till the indignation be accomplished: for that that is determined shall be done. (Daniel 11:27-36)

We commonly think of the Antichrist as just kind of coming along and taking over the world, and we will all live in peace until the last three and a half years of his reign; but Daniel 11:29 tells us that he wages war against the south again. The difference is this time he is resisted and loses heart, then turns away and persecutes the holy ones of God. In the Hebrew, it says that he was grieved and returns to his own land, furious. This tells us that there is war before and after the Antichrist arrives on the scene.

Verse 30 says the ships of Kittim will come against him, and he will lose heart. Typically, we are told that this represents the island of Cyprus, but it seems to me that there is more hidden below the surface than what is seen at first glance. The word "Kittim" means pure ones. These pure ones are none other than the Christians of that day. Therefore, he is enraged at the holy covenant because God showed him up. God's people defeated him in battle. This gives me great hope for God's

The Mark of the Beast

people in the end days. We are not just going to deny that the "off-worlders" are here, but we adapt, get a ship powerful enough to combat this enemy, and we even win for a brief period. Then, the persecution happens like we haven't known before. In that time spoken of in verse 30, we learn that the pure ones shall fall by the sword, be burned alive, go into captivity, or be plundered.

Since Daniel 11 tells us that there is still a king of the North and a king of the South, and that they were hostile, it would be safe to deduce that the kingdoms of the world at this time will not be fully united, and they will not simply give over all their authority to the Antichrist—at first.

In fact, in the first half of Daniel 11, we see that the last king who rises up against the holy ones of God takes his power by deceit. He wasn't born a king.

This deceit is spoken of in Revelation 13. In the first part of Revelation 13, we see that Satan, also referred to as the dragon, summons up the beast with ten horns and seven heads. Thanks to the revelation of Daniel, we know that the beast with its ten horns and seven heads are (represent) four individual kingdoms that produce a total of ten kings, and from the fourth kingdom comes the Antichrist.

The beast comes out of the sea as one beast in Revelation 13. It's important to take notice of this because in Daniel 7:23, we saw that there would be four beast kingdoms. Revelation 13 describes these kingdoms in the same manner but notes that they are all part of the last kingdom. It is my belief that the seven kingdoms will all be under the main serpent leader. I also believe that leader is the multi-headed Leviathan serpent.

God, when giving a dream to Nebuchadnezzar in Daniel 2, used a similar parable to describe four kingdoms that would rule and reign until the last kingdom came, which had the feet of clay and iron. Daniel explained that each of the parts of the body were gold, silver, bronze, and clay, and were different kingdoms. John describes the four beast kingdoms in the same manner. We can even deduce from the fact that the two feet would have ten toes, that this dream even included the ten kings that surrender their power to the Antichrist.

Chapter 15: The Four Kingdoms Become One

The reason he describes it this way, and was shown it this way in heaven, is because it lets us know that the kings come from the same kingdom. They all originate from one source, even though they appear to be different. This is made even more clear to us in Daniel 11.

In Daniel 11:3-4, there is one king, and another revolts against Greece. As a result of this, his kingdom is divided. Then we see the king of the South rising and becoming strong. From this king, one of his princes will rise and become strong as well. The daughter of the king of the South, her envoy, and her father are given up, and then another from her family arises. The king of the North's son rises and causes strife.

We also see in Daniel 11 that the king of the South is immensely powerful and is very hated. It says that several kings lead revolts against the king of the South, including violent men of Daniel's own people. I think it would be safe to reason that each of these kings, especially the king of the South that comes up after the murder of his family, will be antichrist in nature. Many will probably believe that each of these kings is the Antichrist.

However, a new king who is not a king by birth will arise. He isn't even born with the title of king. To be fair, the word for king in Hebrew is the same word used for angel and messenger. He rises and becomes the king of the North peaceably. He doesn't fight or cause war to take power, but he is given the kingdom and rises with the help of a few servants.

The end of days is not going to be a time of great peace. It is going to be a time of war, bloodshed, deceit, trickery, all kinds of violence, and multiple kingdoms. The four kingdoms will become ten kingdoms; then those ten kingdoms will surrender their power over to the Antichrist, and they will become one giant (no pun intended) unified kingdom.

Chapter 16: Discerning the Times

A lot is going to happen in the last days. It will be a crazy time for the world. We may not know the exact time that all of this will begin. We will not know the day or the hour that all of this will happen. One thing we do know, however, is that it will take several years after the revelation of the four beast kingdoms for this to occur. Daniel 11 shows us that the kings that lord over the divided world will have children, and their children will have children.

I have made my own speculations about what will happen at the end of days, based on what I am seeing being pushed on the people of the world. Before I get into any of that, please allow me to give you some Scripture. The first scripture I'd like to show you is Deuteronomy 4:19:

> And lest thou lift up thine eyes unto heaven, and when thou seest the sun, and the moon, and the stars, *even* all the host of heaven, shouldest be driven to worship them, and serve them, which the LORD thy God hath divided unto all nations under the whole heaven.

We see here the word "heaven" is translated as singular in English. However, in Hebrew, it is *ha-shamayim*. This is the plural of the word and means "the heavens." It mentions the sun, the moon, and the stars, and the hosts therein. The word for "hosts" means armies. This scripture

The Mark of the Beast

specifically tells us not to worship the armies from space. This is a huge clue that we could easily miss.

Another key reference in this passage is that it says the LORD your God has divided unto all nations under the whole heaven. In Hebrew, we see the word, *Halaq*, which means divided. When you look at the original text, you see that it says, "Your God has divided them in all manner under the heavens." Therefore, we see all kinds of different mentions in the Bible, and in modernity, that suggest there are multiple forms of Rephaim—hybrids—or what we call "aliens" today.

One could argue, "Well, what about Deuteronomy 17:3, which clearly dictates not to worship the moon or stars? Isn't that what God is talking about in chapter 4?" The answer is, yes; it does say that. However, it also denotes the sun, moon, and stars, and the hosts of the heavens as being separate things that are worshipped.

Now, let's look at Amos:

> Though they dig into hell, from there My hand shall take them; though they climb up to heaven, from there I will bring them down; And though they hide themselves on top of Carmel, from there I will search and take them; though they hide from My sight at the bottom of the sea, from there I will command the serpent, and it shall bite them; though they go into captivity before their enemies, from there I will command the sword, and it shall slay them. I will set My eyes on them for harm and not for good. (Amos 9:2-4, NKJV)

Some would speculate that this scripture also is speaking of times that have already come to pass. I don't believe that to be the case. There are some things here that no one has been able to do until recently.

I would like to point out something about the first part of these verses. God says, "Though they dig into hell." In my mind, I want to try to rationalize this as meaning they dig deep into the earth and create a type of underground bunker. That is logical because people do have bunkers that go miles underground. The Hebrew word for hell is *sheol*,

Chapter 16: Discerning the Times

which also means "into the grave." This could just be a euphemism meaning they dig deep into the earth.

I can't completely reconcile this verse as merely being a euphemism. The reason I saw this is because of the book of Revelation.

> Then the fifth angel sounded: And I saw a star fallen from heaven to the earth. To him was given the key to the bottomless pit. And he opened the bottomless pit, and smoke arose out of the pit like the smoke of a great furnace. So, the sun and the air were darkened because of the smoke of the pit. Then out of the smoke locusts came upon the earth. And to them was given power, as the scorpions of the earth have power. (Revelation 9:1-3, NKJV)

As you can see from this passage, a star is thrown from the heavens with a key, and this looses hell on earth. You also see in this scripture that these locusts have a king who is Abbadon, or Apollyon. The word *Abaddon* in Hebrew means destruction.

For instance, referring to Amos 9:2, God says, "Though they climb up to heaven, from there I will bring them down." The word for "climb" is *yaalu*, which means to climb or to ascend. It is used 888 times in the Bible, and each time it indicates being lifted up, carried up, offered up, climbing up, ascending, and occasionally, withdrawing. We also see the word *hasammayim* used as heaven, however, that is the plural version of the word, which means the heavens, or space.

I believe this could be a reference to the fact that the beast kings that arise from the sea will consider themselves to be gods. The name *Apollyon* references the Greek god Apollo, who is the destroyer or god of death. If you will also notice, the four winds (four spirits) of Revelation 9 and Daniel 7 are loosed in Revelation 9 after this king and his armies come on the earth and wage war against mankind. It's after this that the four angels/winds/spirits are loosed, which stir up the waters and allow the four kingdoms to appear on the earth.

Since it is said that the king of the abyss and the locusts come up from the abyss as the result of a star falling from the heavens, this leads

The Mark of the Beast

me to believe that it could be an indication of how the beast kingdom arises. It also leads me to believe that there is a possibility that a person can access the spirit realm from the natural world. This could suggest some form of interdimensional travel, but I haven't read anything in Scripture yet that shows us this is a possibility.

The evidence is that Elijah was taken up into heaven by God before he died, as had Enoch ascended, and Jesus was taken up alive as well after He was resurrected and returned for forty days and preached the gospel. It would appear that God is the One who controls when, why, and for what purpose the spirit realm can be manifested on the earth.

As of today, the Bible tells us that there are at least three people that are alive in the flesh in heaven. This fact of Scripture rules out the idea that the spirit realm and the physical cannot interact in a tangible manner.

Satan has a counterfeit of almost everything that God has. For example, God can take a person from point A to point B in an instant. We see this very clearly in John 6:21, which says, "Then they willingly received Him into the ship: and immediately the ship was at the land whither they went."

At one time, this type of teleportation was something only seen in the Bible. Then it started appearing in TV shows in the 1960s and later. Today, scientists have successfully utilized quantum teleportation to teleport a particle from earth to a satellite in space. This doesn't mean they are deconstructing humans and sending them to space like some science fiction show, but it may just be the beginning of something remarkably similar.

Returning to Amos 9:2, the next word I'd like to discuss is used in verse 2 for "heaven." The word used is *ha-samayim*. There are two things to note about this word. The first is that ha (he) is used as a prefix meaning "the." The second is that the word is ended in the plural tense with the letters "im." To accurately translate this, it would say, "the heavens." This same expression is used to describe the descendants of Abraham in Genesis 26:4:

Chapter 16: Discerning the Times

> I will make your descendants as numerous as the stars in the sky, and I will give them all these lands, and through your offspring all nations of the earth will be blessed. (NIV)

The word for "stars of the sky" is *kokab ha-samayim* (stars of the heavens/sky). What God is saying in Amos 9 is that even though they try to climb into the heavens, He will bring them down. That is a direct reference to space.

It wasn't until the last century that mankind has been able to ascend into the heavens, or so we are told by a world government that seems to purposefully obfuscate mankind's history. I believe that this is a prophetic indicator that at the end of days, people will be able to climb into space and even live in space, potentially. As of right now, we have just a few people living in space on the space station (that we are aware of). A hundred years ago, we would have considered this passage to be nothing more than a figure of speech; but by today's standards, it's perfectly rational to think that in the near future, we could be living in the heavens (space).

The next part of this scripture that stands out is, "Though they hide from My sight at the bottom of the sea, from there I will command the serpent, and it shall bite them." The word used for "the bottom" means "the floor." This literally says that even if you hide on the sea floor, I will send My serpent to bite you.

The word for "serpent" used in Amos 9:3 is *ha-nahash*. This is the same word used to describe the serpent in the book of Genesis. I believe this could very well be Leviathan, which is discussed in Job 41, or even potentially the serpent from the garden of Eden.

Though the first functional submarine was considered to have been built by Cornelis Jacobszoon Drebbel around 1620, it wasn't until recently that human beings began to have the ability to live under water for long periods of time. To date, there are now people that have small buildings, are living in submarines, or are designing entire cities that can allow human beings to exist at the bottom of the sea.

The Mark of the Beast

Since it is possible for human beings to live in the heavens, deep in the earth, or deep in the ocean, it isn't a stretch of the imagination at all that there could be a civilization of demons hidden deep in the sea, or possibly even hidden in the unseen world that exists around us.

Another scripture I have studied is Deuteronomy 30:4. This verse is interesting. It says, "If *any* of thine be driven out unto the outmost *parts* of heaven, from thence will the LORD thy God gather thee, and from thence will he fetch thee."

Once again, we see the use of the word *ha-shamyim*: the heavens. This states that there is a possibility that the descendants of Israel could somehow be driven out or taken out to the farthest reaches of the heavens.

Given all the Scripture we've seen about the heavens, weapons of indignation coming from the heavens, and man climbing to the heavens, and so forth, I think it would be reasonable to speculate that God is most likely giving a warning of things to come. He almost always associates these times with some great wickedness and rebellion against Him. He equates it with worshipping false idols; and then there is, yet again, a dispersion of His people into space.

I could point you to all the scriptures that everyone knows, such as 2 Timothy, Jude, or other books in the Bible that describe the end of days. Each generation believed that they were the generation that was the fulfillment of those scriptures. Each generation gets a little worse than the one before.

However, to truly discern the times, you need to look at the scriptures that I have laid before you and consider how and when these things are possible. Weigh them for yourself and come to your own conclusions. It's okay if you don't agree with me, but you'd better have your scriptures in the proper context and have done the research for yourself.

Here's how I have seen the end times playing out. The media has been telling us that there are alien life forms out there. They have been trying to implant into our heads that it's foolish to think there would only be one planet in the whole universe that has life on it, that God

Chapter 16: Discerning the Times

personally handcrafted. There have been several "sightings" of UFOs and reports of supposed abductions.

As I said, the devil is not stupid. He is trying to pull the wool over the eyes of humanity. If we just saw a large ship come up out of the sea, and suddenly, we are being attacked by creatures for five months as we are told will happen in the Bible, people would recognize this as the beast spoken of in the book of Revelation, with ease.

Instead, he will come to you as an "intelligent" lifeform and explain that humans came from "alien" DNA, and all life on earth resembles these creatures because the alien DNA split somehow, and that is why these "beings" look like beasts and humans.

These beasts will have the ability to fly. As Daniel describes what he saw in his vision, the goats cross the earth without touching the ground. No wonder they have no problem destroying the earth with fire and plagues. They don't have to live down here and deal with the consequences of their actions—but we do.

They will tell us that they are the gods that were worshipped in the old days, and they will try to convince men that if they do as they are instructed and live lifestyles that are not honoring to God, sacrifice people, or otherwise practice their craft, they can have the same powers as them. This will, however, just be Rephaim hybrids leading humanity into immorality and witchcraft.

These "alien" lifeforms will perform many false miracles, signs, and wonders. They will have followers that go out and do the same thing. They will call down fire, perform false healings, cast out devils, and otherwise try to convince humanity that they are gods, and we can be like them too. They will blaspheme God and the holy ones while attempting to turn the whole world against us, just as the world has been trying to do to this day.

They will have children with the women of this world, but they will not marry them. They will intermingle their seed with women's seed and start to populate the earth with more hybrid seed. The only people that will not be deceived by this great deception are the holy ones of God, and even then, many that will be deceived by this great lie will fall

The Mark of the Beast

to the intensity of its convincing nature. This is why the false prophet will become enraged. He will convince the world to give him supreme rule over the entire world, and then persecute Christians in a fit of rage.

Folks, the end times are not going to be pretty. It isn't going to be fun. There will be war. There will be chaos. There will be crazy things happening that we won't believe. Many people will perish as a result of war after war that nearly destroy the entire world.

> Woe to you who desire the day of the Lord! For what good is the day of the Lord to you? It will be darkness, and not light. It will be as though a man fled from a lion, and a bear met him! Or as though he went into the house, leaned his hand on the wall, and a serpent bit him! Is not the day of the Lord darkness, and not light? Is it not very dark, with no brightness in it? (Amos 5:18-20)

Folks, there isn't anything wrong with wanting to be with the Lord. But you'd better check yourselves when you pray for the end of days to come, because it will be a terrible time. It's very important to start living as holy as you can right now because these "aliens" (though we know that they are actually just human hybrids, and not aliens) will be very convincing and will entice you to sin if you do not submit to the Lord now. You need to start living pure and holy lives today!

This is not a joke. You may scoff, mock, ridicule, and try to defame me for sharing this with you, but the Lord will not be mocked. With this in mind, please read Romans 12:1 again:

> Therefore, I exhort you, brothers, through the compassions of God, to present your bodies as a living sacrifice, holy to God, well-pleasing, which is your reasonable service.

Be blessed and take these words to heart.

Chapter 17: The Time and Weapons of His Indignation

For ages, God has left clues in His Word—which is millennia ahead of scientific breakthrough. For example, God told Noah to build a boat to withstand the rain before there was even rain. He told him the exact measurements that would be needed to house all the animals He was sending to be saved in the ark. There was no such thing as a boat at that time.

> Isaiah 40:22 says, "God sits above the circle of the earth" (NLT). This was stated at a time when people in various parts of the world believed the world was flat.

> Proverbs 8:27 states, "When he prepared the heavens, I *was* there: when he set a compass upon the face of the depth."

> Job 26:10 declares, "He has inscribed a circle on the face of the waters at the boundary between light and darkness." (ESV)

> Job 22:14 talks about the roundness of the earth: "Thick clouds *are* a covering to him, that he seeth not; and he walketh in the circuit of heaven."

The Mark of the Beast

Job 36:27 unfolds the evaporation cycle: "For he maketh small the drops of water: they pour down rain according to the vapour thereof:"

Job 28:5 declares the earth's core is fire: "*As for* the earth, out of it cometh bread: and under it is turned up as it were fire."

Psalm 102 tells us that the universe and everything in it are breaking down and deteriorating.

The first 144 digits of Pi add up to 666. I don't believe this is a coincidence, because the 144,000 that are sealed are mentioned in the last book of the Bible—the book of Revelation—where the mark of the beast is mentioned. It's not just a random chance that God uses these specific numbers together. It is God saying that this is a mark of the time.

In 1 Kings 7:23, we see a similar pattern where Pi is implemented into God's design. We see this in the word *qaveh*. This word has an extra letter in it. Typically, the word is spelled *qof he* (pronounced similar to coffee). In 1 Kings 7:23, it is spelled *qof, vav, hey*. If you take the numerical value of both words and add them, you get 100+6 and 100+6+5. That's 106 and 111. Multiply that number by three for the trinity, or three because there is an extra letter in *qavah*, and you get 3.14150..., which is astonishingly close to Pi.

With these things in mind, is it really that hard to believe that God is aware of all the technological advances we have made? He knows what was, what is, and what will come. He knows all the science that we haven't discovered yet—from astral physics, quantum physics, nuclear science, biological breakthroughs, to new laws which redefine our current understanding of physics, time, and space.

There is no doubt in my mind that God knew what would happen at the end of days and has been forewarning us of it since the book of Genesis. This is shown by His words declaring the earth to be round, that it is suspended as if by nothing, that He knew of the water-vapor cycle and how it creates precipitation, and the fact that it says (or at

Chapter 17: The Time and Weapons of His Indignation

least heavily suggests) there is, in fact, a race of beings that exists in the distant reaches of the heavens, or as we would call it today: outer space.

There is clearly technology from our ancient ancestors. There is clear understanding of the sun, moon, the stars, astronomical alignment, advanced mathematics—and more to be discovered—not only in the annals of history, but also within the pages of the Bible itself, as we have already discussed.

I spent the latter part of this book leading up to this chapter. Now I intend to discuss what we can expect to see at the end of days and identify the times and weapons of God's indignation.

First, let's establish what the days of His indignation are. Simply put, it is referring to the end of days. The word *Zaam* in Hebrew is the word for indignation. It means to be enraged, angered, or indignation. Webster defines *indignation* as anger mingled with contempt, disgust or abhorrence. [8]

The end of days is the time of God's final indignation; this time is also known as the great day of the Lord, or something similarly described.

One of the most key scriptures we see referring to His indignation and the day of His wrath is in Isaiah 13:5-9:

> They come from a far country, from the end of heavens, even the LORD, and the weapons of his indignation, to destroy the whole land. Howl ye; for the day of the LORD is at hand; it shall come as a destruction from the Almighty. Therefore, shall all hands be faint, and every man's heart shall melt: And they shall be afraid: pangs and sorrows shall take hold of them; they shall be in pain as a woman that travaileth: they shall be amazed one at another; their faces shall be as flames. Behold, the day of the LORD cometh, cruel both with wrath and fierce anger, to lay the land desolate: and he shall destroy the sinners thereof out of it.

---

8. Webster's Collegiate Dictionary, s.v. "indignation," (Sparingfield, Mass: G.C. Merriam Co., 1913). 436.

The Mark of the Beast

The reason I included verses 5-8 in this is to point toward what will happen in the final days as well as establish that these events are referring to end-of-day's events.

These so-called "aliens" are human beings that were dispersed into space at the time of the great rebellion of Nimrod. We see evidence of this in Genesis 11, hidden in the verses about building bricks that can send a team of men to space. We also see a reference to this hidden in Deuteronomy 4:19, which we read in the previous chapter:

> And lest thou lift up thine eyes unto heaven, and when thou seest the sun, and the moon, and the stars, *even* all the host of heaven, shouldest be driven to worship them, and serve them, which the LORD thy God hath divided unto all nations under the whole heaven.

At face value, it appears that God is simply saying that we shouldn't worship the sun, the moon, the stars, and the host in the heavens. This is what it's saying, but the word "host" is a word many overlook as simply referring to the stars. We typically think of a host as being a person who entertains guests in some manner. Again, the Bible uses the word "host" to mean army or armies.

If you read this with the knowledge that God is saying, "When you look to the heavens (space), and when you see the sun, the moon, and the stars, and all the armies of the heavens (space), there is no question that it clearly denotes He is speaking of outer space.

This is more than just the planets and stars in outer space, or angel armies.

> And it shall come to pass in that day, that the LORD shall punish the host of the high ones that are on high, and the kings of the earth upon the earth. And they shall be gathered together, as prisoners are gathered in the pit, and shall be shut up in the prison, and after many days shall they be visited. Then the moon shall be confounded, and the sun ashamed, when the LORD of hosts shall reign in

Chapter 17: The Time and Weapons of His Indignation

mount Zion, and in Jerusalem, and before his ancients gloriously. (Isaiah 24:21-23)

The word *ha-marowm* is used in verse 21. This is translated as "high ones" or "elevated," but it is actually a reference to altitude. Therefore, this is referring to the armies that have a high altitude. To me, this is a reference to the hosts of the heavens.

One must question why God would punish the hosts of the heavens if they were just stars and planets in space. Why would God gather all the stars together and punish them in the pit forever? The answer is that He isn't going to punish the planets and stars. He is going to judge those who live in the heavens. He's going to judge the armies of the heavens—the armies of space—and the people.

The next part that we need to look at is the phrase, "have divided unto all the nations." It says, "has given as a heritage." This word is interesting; it is the word *ha-laq*. This is translated as "a heritage," but it actually is defined as "to divide." The reason I believe this is key is because it is reminiscent of when God divided all the tongues of the people at the Tower of Babel. This shows that, at that time, He divided the tongues of the people. The literal translation reads as: "Continuing; Yahweh, your God (*eloheka*); *lekol* (in all manner); every nation (*ha-ammim*)." The next word is important as well. It is *tahat*. This word translates as "under." To simply say "under" is lacking luster. What this word is implying is to be placed under subjection.

It's important to understand that the day of the Lord's indignation is not a term that is solely used to describe the end times. This is a term that is also used to imply that a great wrath is being loosed, which brings great destruction because mankind has turned against God—abandoned His laws, worshipped idols, and withheld justice from the people. With all of this in mind, we can now begin to understand what the phrase, "the weapons of His indignation," means.

By this point, we may have already figured out that they seem to come from the farthest reaches of the heavens, which is the Hebrew way of saying "the skies" or "space." We see this term in Isaiah 13:5.

The Mark of the Beast

This same term is used in Jeremiah 50:25:

> The LORD hath opened his armory, and hath brought forth the weapons of his indignation: for this is the work of the Lord GOD of hosts in the land of the Chaldeans.

It appears that the Lord had raised up an army to deal with Babylon, and those were His weapons of indignation at that time.

Isaiah 13 tells us that the Lord set apart, or consecrated, these weapons for His purpose at the end of days. This means that God is saying this is what the world deserves for wandering away from Him and sinning to the extent that the world will be at in that day. At no other time did He destroy the entire world and unleash such devastation on people as He does in the coming day of His great indignation. The flood was devastating, but these days are going to be much worse.

> For then shall be great tribulation, such as was not since the beginning of the world to this time, no, nor ever shall be. (Matthew 24:21)

These weapons of His indignation are not angels. Many assume these are angels that the Lord set apart to bring about the destruction of the world, because it says they come from the farthest reaches of the heavens. However, if we read the rest of Isaiah 13, we see some things that clearly indicate these are not angels.

> Every one that is found shall be thrust through; and every one that is joined *unto them* shall fall by the sword. Their children also shall be dashed to pieces before their eyes; their houses shall be spoiled, and their wives ravished. Behold, I will stir up the Medes against them, which shall not regard silver; and *as for* gold, they shall not delight in it. T*heir* bows also shall dash the young men to pieces; and they shall have no pity on the fruit of the womb; their eyes shall not spare children. (Isaiah 13:15-18)

Chapter 17: The Time and Weapons of His Indignation

The most horrifying part of this is seeing that in the last days, these weapons of indignation have no regard for human life. It says they will dash babies to pieces. Another thing that devastates me is that their women will be ravished. Typically, this term means to be raped, but it also implies that the women would be carried away as some sort of prize or trophy.

The first time I read this, I was sick to my stomach for weeks. I asked the Lord to please spare me and my family from having to live through this. If none of this happened to me or my family, I still wouldn't want to see it happen to anyone else's family.

For some reason, probably because of the propaganda spread by Hollywood, people largely think that a race of extra-terrestrial beings will be friendly and help advance our civilization with technology, etc. However, the Bible paints a different picture.

We see that they rape women, kill children in the streets, tear open women's wombs, and dash those babies to pieces in the streets. Men are terrified of these beasts. There is war after war. There are plagues, famines, diseases we haven't known, and the sun and stars stop shining and go out. People will be forced to receive a mark that changes their DNA and causes them to get boils on their faces, etc. All of this because these hybrids, or weapons of indignation, will be exposed to the world at the end of days.

Another thing that we will see coming back is slavery. This is something that concerns me. We see this mentioned in Revelation at least two times. Revelation 13:10 very clearly states:

> He that leadeth into captivity shall go into captivity: he that killeth with the sword must be killed with the sword. Here is the patience and the faith of the saints.

We also see a reference to this that perplexes me. This is found in Revelation 18:13:

> And cinnamon, and odours, and ointments, and frankincense, and wine, and oil, and fine flour, and wheat, and

The Mark of the Beast

beasts, and sheep, and horses, and chariots, and slaves, and souls of men.

This is something beyond my comprehension at this time. I understand how you can trade things such as spices, fragrances, foods, and even the part about slavery (I do not condone slavery), but how do you trade souls? How do souls become a commodity at the end of days? Needless to say, the end of days is not going to be a great time.

I have often heard people pray for the Lord to come quickly—for the end of days to come—or they think that we are even in the last of the last days. However, the world is going to become a very dark place. Men will shake with fear; women and children will be treated like nothing. Catastrophes happen in space that cause the sun, moon, and stars to be blacked out.

> Woe unto you that desire the day of the LORD! to what end is it for you? the day of the LORD is darkness, and not light. (Amos 5:18)

Make no mistake, now is the time when we need to be sure to do everything in our power to prevent this. That means we need to pray and be prepared. We need to decide here and now, would we be ready for such events if they were to occur this year? I will delve into how to prepare in a later chapter.

Chapter 18: Leviathan in the Last Days

Leviathan is a beast that we have seen referenced multiple times in the Bible, the most common being in the book of Job. I listed the entire narrative about Leviathan in an earlier chapter. However, I would like to explore the possibilities of Leviathan being involved in the mark of the beast from the beginning of time.

The first time that we hear Leviathan mentioned by name is in the book of Job. It is speculated that the book of Job was written during the 7th Century BC. However, if that were the case, I believe there would be some mention of the Law, the Exodus, Passover, or something along those lines. But there is not.

We also see that Job used the term *qesiytah* as the form of currency of his time. This term is only used three times in the Bible, and that is referring to the time of the patriarchs in Genesis, and in Joshua in a reference to the time of Joseph (a patriarch). Remember this because it will come in handy later in this chapter.

This all leads us to understand that Leviathan has been around as a fearsome, almost mystical creature for ages. Job knew of Leviathan and is speculated to have been alive around 150 to 300 years after the flood. That would mean that Leviathan was around after the flood and most likely somewhere around the time of Nimrod and the Tower of Babel.

The Mark of the Beast

There are a couple of things that we can learn about the serpent from its name. The word "serpent" also means witchcraft, diviner, enchantment, to whisper a spell (as a serpent hisses or whispers), to diligently observe, or to learn by experience. It is my conjecture that this suggests the first witch was none other than the serpent in the garden.

The next thing we learn is that the serpent is not Satan in this scripture. The reason I say this is because it is revealed to us that the serpent was shrewder than any of the living beasts of the field that God had created. Thus, we can deduce that this wasn't an angel in disguise but a creature that was formed on the earth.

We see the mention of a dragon in the book of Revelation. What we usually read is that the serpent is called the diablos and Satan. I am not prone to believe that this is simply what is being said in Revelation 12, because of what we read in Daniel 7 and what we read in the rest of Revelation regarding the serpent.

There are two things that we need to know. Satan is a spirit being; he doesn't have a flesh body. He may be able to manifest in a somewhat solid form, but even when angels manifest and feel tangible, their flesh simply isn't the same as human flesh. They don't bleed, and they don't die. However, if we are to believe that the serpent is Satan, then we must assume that he has a flesh body that somehow transubstantiated from spirit to human, and that parts of him can be wounded, even to death. Satan doesn't die physically. It says in the Bible that it is appointed for all men to die. Satan is not a man; he is a fallen angel.

The dragon is referred to multiple times in the book of Revelation. The part I want to focus on right now is Revelation 12:7-17:

> And there was war in heaven: Michael and his angels fought against the dragon; and the dragon fought and his angels and prevailed not; neither was their place found any more in heaven. And the great dragon was cast out, that old serpent, called the Devil, and Satan, which deceiveth the whole world: he was cast out into

Chapter 18: Leviathan in the Last Days

the earth, and his angels were cast out with him. And I heard a loud voice saying in heaven, Now is come salvation, and strength, and the kingdom of our God, and the power of his Christ: for the accuser of our brethren is cast down, which accused them before our God day and night. And they overcame him by the blood of the Lamb, and by the word of their testimony; and they loved not their lives unto the death. Therefore rejoice, *ye* heavens, and ye that dwell in them. Woe to the inhabiters of the earth and of the sea! for the devil is come down unto you, having great wrath, because he knoweth that he hath but a short time.

And when the dragon saw that he was cast unto the earth, he persecuted the woman which brought forth the man *child*. And to the woman were given two wings of a great eagle, that she might fly into the wilderness, into her place, where she is nourished for a time, and times, and half a time, from the face of the serpent. And the serpent cast out of his mouth water as a flood after the woman, that he might cause her to be carried away of the flood. And the earth helped the woman, and the earth opened her mouth, and swallowed up the flood which the dragon cast out of his mouth. And the dragon was wroth with the woman, and went to make war with the remnant of her seed, which keep the commandments of God, and have the testimony of Jesus Christ.

Verse 9 had me confounded for a while. The cherubim are not described as dragons. I reread verse 9 time and time again. Finally, after much praying in the Spirit, I came up with a theory that seems plausible. I would like to specify that this is my hypothesis, not necessarily a revelation from God. I am open to discussion, and I am sure that I will learn more as time goes on. As all hypotheses go, it is not a law or a doctrine.

The Mark of the Beast

In Greek, we see a couple of things that I believe will change how we interpret the end-time revelation John gave to us. Number one: the serpent, the dragon, and diablos.

> And the great dragon was cast out, that old serpent, called the Devil, and Satan, which deceiveth the whole world: he was cast out into the earth, and his angels were cast out with him. (Revelation 12:9)

When we look at this in Greek, we see what appears to be two different entities being named—possibly three separate beings. It says in Greek, the dragon (the great dragon), the serpent the ancient, called the diablos, and the Satan.

I looked up these words in Greek and studied them for a while. The great dragon and the ancient serpent surprised me. The word for dragon is *drakon*. This is not a surprise to me. It's only a letter's difference from our word "dragon." This is the mega dragon. We see this same terminology used in Ezekiel 29:3 when God has Ezekiel prophesy to the great dragon He calls Pharoah.

The next series of words is "the serpent the ancient." The word for "serpent" here is *opheis* in Greek. This word means serpent. It is used fourteen times in the New Testament, and it always means serpent. It never means Satan. It is not used in reference to Satan. Only one time does it appear to be referring to Satan, (Revelation 12:9), but I do not believe that is the case, because in the rest of Revelation, it is never used in the same sentence as Satan again.

The word for ancient in "the ancient serpent" is *archaios*. This word means the original or the ancient. It's referring to the progenitor of the serpents, or the first serpent (the original serpent).

After this, we see that it begins to speak of Satan by calling him the diablos, the Satan. The diablos and the Satan mean the same thing essentially. The word "diablos" means a traducer, or someone who intentionally makes malicious and slanderous statements against a person in order to defame them, shame them, or expose them. The word *satanas* in Greek is derived from the Hebrew word,

Chapter 18: Leviathan in the Last Days

satan, and means slanderer or accuser. This word is used multiple times in the New Testament to refer strictly to Satan. Only one time are the words dragon and serpent used in the same sentence as Satan in the New Testament. Not one time in the Old Testament is Satan ever called a serpent.

We get this idea that the serpent in the garden was Satan because that's what we were taught, but it never actually says that in the New or Old Testament.

After Revelation 12:9, the only mention of Satan with the dragon is in Revelation 20:2. It uses the same terminology as Revelation 12:9, but there is one key difference: The word "autoun" is used when it says, "And he laid hold on the dragon, that old serpent, which is the Devil, and Satan, and bound him a thousand years."

The word *autoun* can mean "him," but it is used nearly 1,500 times to mean "them" or "themselves." So, when it says, "bound him," it could very well mean that they were bound. In fact, if you read on, chapter 20:7 says that Satan is let out of his prison. In this verse, it uses the word *autou* instead of *autoun*. Also, it doesn't mention the serpent or dragon at all. I believe that this is because the dragon and serpent are the Antichrist and the serpent from Eden.

This being said, we find several scriptures about Leviathan being punished and having a part in the end of days. One splendid example is Isaiah 27:1:

> In that day the LORD with his sore and great and strong sword shall punish leviathan the piercing serpent, even leviathan that crooked serpent; and he shall slay the dragon that *is* in the sea.

This is pretty straightforward. The term "on that day" is b*a-yom*. This means "the coming day" or "in that day," which is an indication of things to come. This term is often used when describing the end of days. This verse tells us there is a day yet to come when Leviathan will be punished. We see another reference to Leviathan in Ezekiel 29:3:

The Mark of the Beast

> Speak, and say, Thus saith the Lord GOD; Behold, I am against thee, Pharaoh king of Egypt, the great dragon that lieth in the midst of his rivers, which hath said, My river is mine own, and I have made it for myself.

We see this same mentality mentioned in Job 40 as well, when God is describing the behemoth to Job. Then, in the next chapter, God describes Leviathan. I believe the two are one and the same.

Interestingly enough, God calls the behemoth a piercing serpent in Job 40. The word *beriah,* used to describe Leviathan as a fleeing serpent in Isaiah 27, can also mean piercing.

Another key takeaway from Ezekiel 29 is that Leviathan is called the Pharoah of Egypt. It is said that this Pharoah is a great dragon that lives in the midst of the river. That river is the Nile. The takeaway here is that Job 42 mentions using *kesitah. Kesitah* is mentioned three times in the Bible, and each time it refers to the time of the patriarchs in an area (Hebron) that was part of Egypt. This tells me that the great dragon that lived in the river was most likely the behemoth in Job 40, and its description is very similar to Leviathan in Job 41.

In Genesis 1:21, we are told that God created the great sea creatures. The words used here are *ha-tannim ha-gadolim*: the dragons greats (great dragons) of the sea. In these passages, in correlation with Job 40, we get an understanding that God created Leviathan in Genesis before He created man. Separately, it would be my assumption that Leviathan (perhaps there are multiple according to Genesis 1:21) is the one responsible for the crossbreeding of the animals that created what we call dinosaurs today. Before Darwin published his demonic theory of evolution, the dinosaurs were all called dragons.

Another scripture is Psalm 74:14:

> Thou brakest the heads of leviathan in pieces, *and* gavest him *to be* meat to the people inhabiting the wilderness.

Chapter 18: Leviathan in the Last Days

This scripture pertains to the end of days as well. We see this in the book of Daniel 8:23 when the Antichrist is mentioned:

> And in the latter time of their kingdom, when the transgressors are come to the full, a king of fierce countenance, and understanding dark sentences, shall stand up.

The word for "fierce countenance" is *panim*. That is the plural Hebrew word meaning "faces." This shows us that the creature mentioned here doesn't just have one head but seems to have multiple heads.

Interestingly, the seven heads and ten horns of the beast stand for seven continents and ten kings, but the beast itself stands for that end-time beast that comes up from the sea. This is an important aspect. Remember, God crushed the heads of Leviathan. It also says in Psalm 104:24-25:

> So is this great and wide sea, wherein are things creeping innumerable, both small and great beasts. There go the ships: there is that leviathan, whom thou hast made to play therein.

This shows us that Leviathan is multiheaded, and it seems to reside in the sea. This is probably one of the only "dinosaurs" that God created. There may be more, but this one seems to be one that He made in the beginning, and it resided within Eden. I believe this is the original serpent mentioned in Revelation 12.

One thing that stands out to me, regarding this serpent, comes from Revelation 12:17. I mentioned this before, but the dragon went after the woman. It's doesn't say that Satan went after the woman; it was the dragon. If you recall, it says the dragon warred with the seed of the woman and uses the word meta. This means to alter or change. This further drives me to believe that the end-time dragon of

The Mark of the Beast

Revelation is Leviathan, and is the serpent from the garden, because it was at enmity or war with the seed of the woman.

> And I will put enmity between thee and the woman, and between thy seed and her seed; it shall bruise thy head, and thou shalt bruise his heel. (Genesis 3:15)

The serpent, Leviathan, the red dragon, whatever you choose to call it from this point forward, has been chasing after and trying to destroy the seed of woman ever since Genesis 3:15. It is my belief that this beast will not stop until he is chained in hell upon the return of Jesus.

Chapter 19: Leviathan and Typhon

In the previous chapter, we discussed how Leviathan is more likely to be a serpent, and even more so to be the serpent from the garden of Eden that caused mankind to be cast out of paradise. Now let's take a look at how Leviathan has manifested itself in the past.

When I first began writing this book, I didn't understand how flesh beings could go from earth to hell. However, the Lord reminded me that the earth swallowed up Korah and his companions.

> And it came to pass, as he had made an end of speaking all these words, that the ground clave asunder that *was* under them: and the earth opened her mouth, and swallowed them up, and their houses, and all the men that *appertained* unto Korah, and all *their* goods. They, and all that *appertained* to them, went down alive into the pit, and the earth closed upon them: and they perished from among the congregation. (Numbers 16:31-33)

This shows me that it is possible for people that are alive here and now to enter the spirit realm while they are still living. I cannot imagine that this is something a human being would want to do, because

The Mark of the Beast

demons in hell only want to tear humans to pieces. But those that are hybrids—and have become like the hell-bound hybrids—may have a better time in hell. That's my own speculation based on eyewitness testimonies I have heard from people that have been to hell.

We see this very same thing happening at the end of days as the angel blows the fifth trumpet:

> And the fifth angel sounded, and I saw a star fall from heaven unto the earth: and to him was given the key of the bottomless pit. And he opened the bottomless pit; and there arose a smoke out of the pit, as the smoke of a great furnace; and the sun and the air were darkened by reason of the smoke of the pit. And there came out of the smoke locusts upon the earth: and unto them was given power, as the scorpions of the earth have power. And it was commanded them that they should not hurt the grass of the earth, neither any green thing, neither any tree; but only those men which have not the seal of God in their foreheads. And to them it was given that they should not kill them, but that they should be tormented five months: and their torment *was* as the torment of a scorpion, when he striketh a man. And in those days shall men seek death, and shall not find it; and shall desire to die, and death shall flee from them.
>
> And the shapes of the locusts *were* like unto horses prepared unto battle; and on their heads *were* as it were crowns like gold, and their faces *were* as the faces of men. And they had hair as the hair of women, and their teeth were as *the teeth* of lions. And they had breastplates, as it were breastplates of iron; and the sound of their wings *was* as the sound of chariots of many horses running to battle. And they had tails like unto scorpions, and there were stings in their tails: and their power *was* to hurt men five months. And they had a king over them, *which is* the angel of

Chapter 19: Leviathan and Typhon

the bottomless pit, whose name in the Hebrew tongue *is* Abaddon, but in the Greek tongue hath *his* name Apollyon. (Revelation 9:1-11)

Notice how the beasts that came out of hell are *chimera* that are mixed with different beasts and human beings as well. There is a demon army that is actually loosed from within hell into the world. That is terrifying. They will not have any remorse or hesitation to do their best to harm humanity. The demons in hell are the seed of the serpent, and they absolutely hate humanity.

Take note of who the king of hell is, or who the king of these beasts is. He is called Abbadon or Apollyon. *Abbadon* and *Apollyon* are both words that mean destruction in Hebrew and Greek. There are two gods that fit this description (probably more if I were to guess) that are called gods of destruction. That is Set (Egyptian God) and a god named Typhon (Greek God).

"Typhon," which is where we get the word "typhoon" from, is a god that is a said to be a storm giant. He is said to have multiple heads and a serpent's body with the torso of a human. It is said that lightning came from him, fire issued forth from his mouth, heads in the form of a bear, lion, bull, and a leopard.

According to Greek mythos, he laid seige to heaven but was defeated by Zeus. Typhon was believed to be responsible for great tempests and storms that he brought forth from hell itself. (Does that resemble any of the descriptions of the dragon that emerges from the sea at the end of days?)

Human embellishment and demonic twisting are added to all of these stories of the ancient gods. I can see here what is most likely extra, but I can also see that some of these attributes mirror Leviathan from the Bible. For example:

> His sneezings flash forth light, And his eyes *are* like the eyelids of the morning. Out of his mouth go burning lights; sparks of fire shoot out. Smoke goes out of his nostrils, as *from* a boiling pot and burning rushes.

The Mark of the Beast

> His breath kindles coals, and a flame goes out of his mouth. (Job 41:18-21)

Notice it says that lightning shoots forth from Leviathan's eyes, and Typhon is described as producing storms. I can't speak for you, but when I think of storms, I think of thunder and lightning.

Typhon is also said to have spit fire at the heavens. He thought that he could bring down the gods by boiling fire in his mouth. Notice that it says he has multiple heads as well. The book of Job tells us that Leviathan spits fire, shoots lightning from its eyes, and all that too.

The part that I want to focus on is the fact that this dragon creature is typically described as having a human-like torso. Remember several chapters ago where we discussed the possibility that some sexual sin may have occurred in the garden?

The likelihood that this Typhon serpent is the very same Leviathan spirit is high, in my opinion. It says in Genesis 3:1:

> Now the serpent was more crafty than any beast of the field that the LORD God had made. And he said to the woman, "Did God really say, 'You must not eat from any tree in the garden?'" (BSB)

The word for crafty, or cunning, in some translations, is the Hebrew word *arum*. This word means cunning/crafty. It is used to mean that eleven times. However, it is also used to mean naked nineteen times.

In Genesis 3:15, God curses this Leviathan to eat dust forever. We must also remember that God tells Job that Leviathan can travel between the water and the land:

> His underparts are like sharp pieces of broken pottery; He moves across *and* spreads out [grooves] like a threshing sledge on the mire (muddy river banks). (Job 41:30, AMP)

Chapter 19: Leviathan and Typhon

The serpent is never forgiven. We see this in Isaiah 65. This verse is speaking of a time after Jesus returns, God creates the new heaven and earth, and all is well:

> The wolf and the lamb shall feed together, and the lion shall eat straw like the bullock: and dust *shall be* the serpent's meat. They shall not hurt nor destroy in all my holy mountain, saith the LORD. (Isaiah 65:25)

I wondered what that could mean but couldn't ever put my finger on it until I heard Sam Shamoun, History's most prominent apologist, quote this verse and say, "The serpent remains cursed forever."

After praying about this for a long time, the Lord said, "He is eating the dirt of hell." Me being me, I can't just take what anyone is saying or what I hear in the spirit and accept it. I have to find a scripture and test it. With that little guidepost, I was able to quickly find the scripture that shows that the dust God is speaking about is, in fact, *sheol* (hell):

> If I say to corruption (sheol), 'You *are* my father,'
> And to the worm, 'You *are* my mother and my sister,'
> Where then *is* my hope? As for my hope, who can see it? *Will* they go down to the gates of Sheol? Shall *we have* rest together in the dust? (Job 17:14-16, NKJV)

I believe that the worm that Job is talking about here is the worm of hell, death, and the grave, that consumes the dead flesh of those that are tormented in hell. Jesus describes it like this:

> And if thy foot offend thee, cut it off: it is better for thee to enter halt into life, than having two feet to be cast into hell, into the fire that never shall be quenched: Where their worm dieth not, and the fire is not quenched. (Mark 9:45-46)

The Mark of the Beast

We also see a reference to hell being muddy and dirty in Psalm 40:2:

> He also brought me up out of a horrible pit, out of the miry clay, and set my feet upon a rock, *and* established my steps. (NKJV)

In most of the stories of Typhon, or whatever name he is called in various languages, he is cast into hell by a greater god. One day, however, Typhon will return from hell. According to the Bible, Leviathan will return this same way.

The red dragon (which typhon is described as) emerges from the pit of hell, from deep within the ocean. And what does this dragon begin to do when it comes back? As I stated in a previous chapter, it becomes enraged with "the woman" and begins to alter her seed.

Surely it is not a coincidence that this Typhon serpent and Leviathan share so many similarities. This is something that we need to consider and seek God for more clarity on. I believe we are about to see the original serpent make a comeback. It will be released from the pit of hell, and nothing about it will be better.

Bryan Melvin, author of *A Land Unknown: Hell's Dominion*, told me in an interview that people don't get better in hell. You don't go there and get refined by the fire. He said that people who are there get worse and more sinful.

After considering that statement for a while, it made sense to me. Satan has been going in and out of hell for 6,000 years. He never gets better. He gets worse and worse as time goes on. The demons have been there for thousands of years, and they just go on and on getting worse and worse. They see God. They know He is real. They continue to blaspheme and sin against Him and try to usher in the Antichrist.

When Levithan is loosed from the bonds that are restraining him, he isn't going to be the same perfect serpent that he was in the garden. He is going to have 6,000 years' worth of bitterness and hatred

Chapter 19: Leviathan and Typhon

toward humanity. The evidence is in Revelation 12:7. He wages war with the woman to alter her seed. Not only that, but he will also have had thousands of years to figure out the most deceptive manner in which to deceive the world.

Chapter 20: The Great Deception

I am aware that to many, I may sound like a madman, a heretic, or perhaps some kind of conspiracy theorist. But that doesn't prevent me from feeling the compelling urge of the Lord to share these discoveries with you. My ultimate goal of this entire book is to help bring attention to the coming end-time deception. If I can get through to even one person so that when this all plays out and begins to manifest in a great manner, they don't get the mark, then it was worth it. I will gladly look like a fool to save the one from certain destruction.

The coming great deception is mentioned in the New Testament in 2 Thessalonians 2:11. It reads as such in the King James Version:

> And for this cause God shall send them strong delusion,
> that they should believe a lie.

This verse is of particular interest and helps us to understand why these end-time things are playing out, and it also helps us to recognize that just because God allowed it doesn't mean He is the One responsible for what occurs. Each person is responsible for their own sin.

The phrase "to send" in verse 11 implies something is put forth or allowed to happen. The best term I can think of to describe this is the Latin phrase, "terminus ad quem." The literal translation of this means "up until which." It signifies that this leads up to the end or termination

The Mark of the Beast

of something. This gives us the sense that things are allowed to happen; it is the end of times, and it *will* come to an end.

The next word that captures my attention is the word translated as "strong," which is *energeio*. You may be looking at this word and thinking that it looks like the word "energy." That is actually the derivative of our word "energy." This type of energy is referring to superhuman power or effectual working.

I feel the most important word to understand in this verse is the word "delusion." There's not really a need to delve into the Greek meaning of the word because it is straightforward and means delusion. This is the perfect word to use in this context regarding what is coming in the last days.

Webster defines "delusion" as a misleading of the mind; that which is falsely believed or propagated; a mistaken notion arising from lack of knowledge or from false judgement, usually affecting the real concerns of life.[9]

This is a great indication of what is coming in the last days. There will be great signs and wonders performed by Christians. However, there will be lying signs performed by the false prophets of the beast as well. There will be angels flying through the skies pouring out bowls of wrath and preaching the gospel to all the world. There will be two witnesses in the streets; you will see fire coming from their mouths, and they will stop rains and afflict people who try to attack them—until they are slain in the streets and lay dead for three days, then are resurrected.

At the same time, people will begin to believe that they can become gods. They will believe the lies that the Enemy puts forth declaring they are the gods that created mankind, gave us technology, advanced our civilizations, etc. To be straightforward, I would like to declare to you what exactly I perceive it is that we will see taking place in the very near future.

---

9. Webster's Collegiate Dictionary, s.v. "delusion," (Sparingfield, Mass: G.C. Merriam Co., 1913). 232.

Chapter 20: The Great Deception

The first thing I have noticed about the great deception is that humanity has been being primed for it for years. If we look back on it, there have been references to flying discs in the sky for millennia. However, it's not until recently that mainstream society has begun really entertaining and being fed the idea that there may be life on other planets that are far more civilized than ours.

The first major mention in modern society was the unexplained crash in Roswell, New Mexico, in 1947. There were instances like this where people had seen UFOs, but no one really knew how to explain them. For example, in Fatima, Portugal, there was an instance in which it is believed the sun moved in the sky. They call it the miracle of the sun. However, several witnesses reported that they saw a dull silver disc that was emitting the bright light they were seeing. It was flying up and down and hovering over people's heads within 100 yards of onlookers in certain areas. This was no small deception. Thousands of onlookers saw this happen. There is documentation. There were interviews after the event. There were photographs.

In the past century, we have steadily seen the idea of extra-terrestrial life consuming pop culture, not only in America, but worldwide. Tales of life-forms far more advanced than ours coming to earth and attacking the planet; tales of life in distant galaxies that fight with light swords and magic powers; starships cruising through space exploring new worlds and seeking out new life; little green men initiating first contact with the human race; and, of course, tales of life outside of earth, known to government agencies for ages, yet deliberately obfuscated from the world to maintain peace and prevent the inevitable decline of mankind as they discover the reality that we are not alone in the universe.

To date, there have been movies made that state that life on earth came from some benevolent, advanced, god-like society. There have even been tales that state that mankind was made simply to be slaves to the gods. I won't go into that right now, but I recommend looking into Genesis 2 and the purpose for which God set Adam in the garden of Eden.

Something is going to happen to open the eyes of the world to the fact that there is "life" from places other than the earth. It will most

The Mark of the Beast

likely be a series of cities that have ships appear that are the size of cities or miles wide at least. Perhaps something is visibly seen on a telescope somewhere, or a radio signal is picked up definitively declaring, "You are not alone in the universe."

I feel as though Hollywood has been trying to prepare us for an event remarkably similar. It almost seems as though they have been probing the populace for either the most acceptable way or the most shocking way to reveal this alien agenda.

This great revelation will be a shock to nations as everyone suddenly realizes that "we are not alone." That's exactly what they want you to think.

They will tell the world that they have been here living on the planet for thousands of years, watching humanity, and keeping track. In fact, Jeremiah 4:16-17 mentions the watchers that come from distant lands, using the same terminology as Daniel:

> "Make mention to the nations, yes, proclaim against Jerusalem, that watchers come from a far country and raise their voice against the cities of Judah. Like keepers of a field they are against her all around, because she has been rebellious against Me," says the Lord. (NKJV)

That very same word we see translated as "country" is *arets*. This word was the only word that was used to mean earth. It's most commonly translated as "lands," but it has been my observation that it is speaking of earth or earth-like planets.

It's imperative that we be aware of these things. The great deception will be the revelation that there are "aliens" from other worlds. It will be a very convincing deception. It will appear as though Christians were forewarned, and new agers were forewarned because they will take Scripture and twist it to suit their purpose. They will try to make humanity believe that Scripture was given to the prophets by various aliens in an attempt to prepare us.

Chapter 20: The Great Deception

One major thing that will happen is they will try to say that mankind has perverted "their" words throughout the millennia in order to justify their (human's) own agendas and maintain control over the human race. I find that to be ironic, because this is exactly what is being done by the dark forces that are trying to usher in the end of days as quickly as possible.

The great deception will be painfully obvious to Christians. The Lord will basically rend the heavens to show the world that He is real. He will send His angels in plain sight of mankind to leave the world without any excuse as to why they didn't turn from their sins. The delusion—the great lie—will be so powerful that even in light of these things being done, the people who drink from the delusion of the Antichrist will still shake their fists at God as though He is the bad guy for trying to save them from an eternity of torment in the pits of *Sheol*.

Chapter 21: How to Prepare

The end of days will not be a fun time for anyone. The Enemy knows that his days are numbered, and he is furious about this. From here on out, it is your job to prepare for what is yet to come.

Some people will read this book and think to themselves, "Well, that's it, I need a bunker, and I need to store up beans and rice for the apocalypse." That's not the right attitude to have. As we learned from Amos 9, that will not keep you safe from what is coming. Prepare yourself, because we are about to take a crash course on what we are called to do as Christians.

The number one thing that we need to do to prepare is understand that this is the reality of things to come. If we don't reach the conclusion that aliens are not from another planet and are not who or what they say they are, then we will inevitably fall prey to the coming great deception.

For centuries, the Enemy of God has been working to set up a lie to deceive the world. This lie is that mankind wasn't an accident but was created by "aliens." These beings will even go as far as to tell us they are the *elohim* (gods) that created the heavens and the earth, and that they are the *elohim* that are referenced in Genesis when God said, "Let Us make man in Our image." These lies are just a few of the blasphemies that will be spoken out of the mouths of these creatures.

It is said that there will be lying signs and wonders, many miracles, etc., at this time. We must begin to accept that God is all-powerful and

The Mark of the Beast

understand the authority that we have been given by Him. This may not seem important, but I have observed that, for centuries, many denominations completely abandon the idea that God still speaks, that He does signs and wonders, that He heals, and that we are called to cast out demons and do all the exploits of the Bible. Because of this, I have seen countless men and women leave the church and pursue the devil, pursue new age, and pursue different demonic avenues of power.

God is the same yesterday, today, and forevermore; He never changes. If God spoke in AD 75 to the apostles to authenticate His Word, then He still speaks today to authenticate His Word. If God healed someone in AD 40 under the hands of Peter and John, then God still heals today. Anything that God did thousands of years ago, He still does today. To say that God doesn't do these things is to deny the Word of God and declare His Word to be false. When you make God a liar, it is easy to fall into sin and wander away from the only path of enlightenment.

It is my conjecture that one of the lying signs that will be performed by these beings is to bring life to an inanimate statue. We see this in Revelation 13:15:

> And he had power to give life unto the image of the beast, that the image of the beast should both speak, and cause that as many as would not worship the image of the beast should be killed.

This seems to me to be a counterfeit of the Genesis account and how God brought about the creation of Adam. He made Adam out of clay, sculpted him with His hands, and then breathed a blast of life into his nostrils. In Revelation 13, the word for life is *pneuma*. That word means "spirit." In Genesis 1, the word for breath is *ruach*, which means breath, life, air, or spirit.

Many are already Christians that are reading this book, but some are not allowing Christ to be the true Lord of their life. Making Him the Lord of your life simply means that you need to be sure you are giving Him every area of your life and your heart. Many of us, including myself, fall short in many ways. We must always strive to be closer

Chapter 21: How to Prepare

to the Lord and have an unfailing and unshakeable faith in Him and in His Word.

If you are not a Christian, you need to give your life to Him NOW! We often think this means we have to say a prayer, or we must make a public declaration before all the church somewhere, but the man on the cross simply turned from his old ways and said:

> Lord, remember me when You come into Your kingdom.
> (Luke 23:42, NKJV)

Before this, another of the Gospels tells us that he was mocking Jesus and calling Him names, just like many of the other onlookers. Jesus answered him:

> Truly I tell you, today you will be with Me in paradise.
> (Luke 23:43)

Salvation was as simple as a change of heart toward God's Son. Nevertheless, if you feel like you need or simply desire to say a prayer and dedicate yourself to God, say this aloud:

> *Jesus, I have sinned against You, and I am sorry! I need You in my life! I want You in my life! Please forgive me of my sins. Wash me in Your blood and come live in my heart. I accept You as Lord and Savior of my life.*

If you just said that prayer, then I want you to go to your local church—one that believes in the gifts of the Spirit and the fivefold ministry—and tell them you want to be baptized. If you need a Bible, I am sure they will give you one. If not, you can download one, or contact us at Fireside Grace, and we will help you get a Bible.

Next, I want you to receive the Holy Spirit. There are several ways that you can receive the Holy Spirit. You can go to a pastor that believes in this, and they can lay hands on you, and you can receive. Or you can simply ask the Holy Spirit, and He will come upon you and set you on

The Mark of the Beast

fire. You can also watch a video online and receive an impartation of the Spirit. The choice is yours. God will meet you wherever your faith is at.

You need to read your Bible daily. It is important to stay in the Word of God and read it, study it, and analyze it daily. I came across the revelation in this book partly because God showed me some of it, but mostly because I read the Bible and study the Word diligently so that when someone asks me what I believe, I can respond to any question they ask. Furthermore, it increases the amount of faith in God that I have because I have a greater revelation of His nature and character.

When reading the Bible and studying the Word, it's important to look at different theories or doctrines concerning what you are studying. It's okay to hear someone else's opinion about a topic and agree or disagree with them.

I find that when someone disagrees with a topic that I am discussing, they typically send an e-mail or leave a scathing comment belittling my opinion or questioning my salvation through Jesus Christ. Then they leave a comment about why I am wrong, but they almost never supply Scripture to support their opinion.

I also instruct you to start living a holy life. I am not telling you that you need to wear a headcover when you pray or not wear makeup if you are female. What I am saying is that you need to stop cussing, stop watching inappropriate movies, stop lying, stop gossiping, stop listening to secular music, and so on.

I could give you a list of things that you shouldn't do, but I want to encourage you with the things that you need to do. Submit your heart to God. Delight in Him. Read His Word. Pray for people. Lay hands on the sick. Believe that His words are final. I will let the Lord convict you in any area that you need help.

Take time to pray. Ask the Holy Spirit to reveal His heart to you. Every night before Brandi and I go to bed, we pray. We ask God to reveal His heart to us about what He wants taught to the body of Christ. We also ask Him to show us any area of our heart that needs to change so we can be more like Him.

Chapter 21: How to Prepare

Jesus never fails to show up and tell us what we can do differently to be more like Him. If you humble yourself before Him, you will see a drastic change in your life in a noticeably brief period of time.

Many of us today are aware that there is spiritual warfare happening all around us. However, we just take the Bible at its Word, yet never seem to fathom that there is an actual Enemy letting loose fiery arrows and constructing ramparts and various siege weapons to lay waste to our lives. Thankfully for us, God has promised that no weapon formed against us shall prosper. Nevertheless, that does not mean that just because we cannot see what is happening in the spirit realm (at least most can't), that nothing is happening.

One more thing that we need to be aware of to combat the great deception is understanding what the blasphemy of the Holy Spirit truly is. Most people are taught that blasphemy of the Holy Spirit is giving credit to Satan for something that God has done. When I was a teenager in youth group, I asked my pastor what blasphemy of the Holy Spirit was, and he said exactly that.

My issue with this statement is that almost everyone has blasphemed God in such a manner. I personally blasphemed God and declared that He was the same God as all the other gods; He was just called by a different name. At one point, I believed that God was only as powerful as the people that worshipped Him, because it appeared that the more a nation or people closely adhered to their gods, the more their gods interacted and responded. I was deceived.

I used to mock God and talk about what a joke Jesus was. I partook in witchcraft rituals, talked to demons, and used my God-given gifts to manipulate people and use them for my wants and desires. I was friends with people that straight-up gave glory to Satan in the face of God for something God had done.

Today, my friends and I, and many people I have met through my years of ministry, have been redeemed, and our salvation is assured. There is no doubt in my heart that I have been forgiven and redeemed. I have encountered God, been to the throne room of God, talked face-to-face with Jesus on several occasions, been told by Jesus Himself what

The Mark of the Beast

my purpose is in this world, and I take part in the supernatural daily. For these reasons, I do not agree that blasphemy of the Holy Spirit is simply giving credit to Satan for things that God has done.

I have seen an alternative definition of blasphemy of the Holy Spirit that says it is a hardening of the heart which chooses to remain in sin and ignore the call of the Holy Spirit to repent. This is more accurate than the previous definition, but it is still missing something. Please allow me to elaborate.

It is my belief that the blasphemy of the Holy Spirit goes deeper than just saying something bad about God. It truly is a deep-seated resentment, hatred, and rejection of God, and even more. I believe that the blasphemy of the Holy Spirit is receiving the mark of the beast.

The mark of the beast is not just something that mankind is waiting for that does not exist yet. The mark is something that has existed since approximately 238 years after the fall of man. We see this, as stated in the beginning of the Bible, in Genesis 4, where it says, "They began to call upon the name of God."

The word for "began" means to defile, to wound, to prostitute, to slay. The word for "to call" is *liqro,* and it means to accost, to bewray self, or to betray. In these two words, we see acts that are violent and a betrayal to God and His name. As stated earlier in this book, it is my belief that at this time is when men began to mix their seed with the serpent's seed. I believe that this is part of the blasphemy of the Spirit.

Demons are hybrid spirits. We learn that from Genesis 14, Isaiah 14, and from the origin of the word "demon." "Demon" is derived from the Latin word *daemon,* which hails from the Greek word *daimon* and is the word that was used to describe the demigods or lesser gods in Greek mythology. First Corinthians 10:20 tells us that the gods the heathens are sacrificing to are demons (demigods).

A demigod is a being that is a mortal mixed with a god. I believe that this is a reference to man mixing himself (the Spirit of God within) with an animal and combining their spirits.

We commonly think of the spirit as being its own separate thing, but according to Adam, Jesus, and Paul, when a person has sex with

Chapter 21: How to Prepare

another person, they become one in spirit. When we become Christians, we become one spirit with God, as we have received His seed (*spermata*) into our spirit.

In the dream that Daniel interpreted for Nebuchadnezzar in Daniel 2:43, we see in Hebrew that there is a mixing of something or someone with another (with the seed of men), but they don't cleave to one another. The word for cleave in this verse is *debeq*. This word means marriage. It is first used in Genesis 2:24 when Adam prophesies the first marriage and the future of man before there were other men or marriages.

Make no mistake, folks; the push to engage in sex before marriage is not a coincidence. This is a planned strategy of the Enemy that is leading up to the big revelation of "alien life" that is coming in the years ahead. The idea of getting married will be something that is held onto by a handful of believers, but even now, the world and many in the church reject the idea that sex should only be for the marriage bed.

I will conclude this book with this warning: We are indeed facing perilous times. In the not-so-distant future, we are going to see ships in the sky, panic, hysteria, acceptance, and an abounding of lawlessness.

When I say lawlessness, I don't mean it will be complete anarchy. The biblical idea of lawlessness is when people don't obey the laws of God, but they choose to pursue idols and act as heathens.

Throughout antiquity, there has always been a rule of law for mankind. Whether it was the code of Hammurabi, the laws of the Egyptians, Roman Law, or even today's laws that we have constructed, there has always been law. God considers something to be lawlessness when we choose to disobey His commands.

Jesus said in Matthew 7:21-23:

> Not everyone that saith unto me, Lord, Lord, shall enter into the kingdom of heaven; but he that doeth the will of my Father which is in heaven. Many will say to me in that day, Lord, Lord, have we not prophesied in thy name? and in thy name have cast out devils? and in thy name done many wonderful works? And then will I

The Mark of the Beast

profess unto them, I never knew you: depart from me, ye that work iniquity.

The word for iniquity used in this scripture is *anomia*. It means lawlessness, unrighteous, or wicked. This word comes from the word *anomas* and is a compound of "a," which means against, and the word *onoma*, which means law. Put plainly, it means without law, or lawless. This law that Jesus is referring to is the law of God.

There will indeed be law and order at the time of the return of the hybrids. There will be kings. There will be laws, but they will be laws that benefit the "gods" and cause mankind to turn their back on the God of heaven.

I also believe that we will see a devaluation or dehumanization of pure, five-fingered, unaltered, Christian, human beings. This has been a pattern that we have seen perpetrated by people influenced by the demonic to justify eugenics and genocide. The most notable of these genocides would be the Holocaust as perpetrated by Hitler through the dehumanization of the Jews in the 1930s and '40s. This same devaluation of human life is how America has justified abortion for so many years. It is the dehumanization of a baby's life in order to perpetrate the mass holocaust of unborn children, also known as abortion.

Let me remind you of the example of this in Isaiah 13. In verse 5, we see that God says His weapons of indignation come from the farthest reaches of space. In the same chapter, we read:

> Their children also shall be dashed to pieces before their eyes; their houses shall be spoiled, and their wives ravished. Behold, I will stir up the Medes against them, which shall not regard silver; and as for gold, they shall not delight in it. Their bows also shall dash the young men to pieces; and they shall have no pity on the fruit of the womb; their eyes shall not spare children. (Isaiah 13:16-18)

I know that I shared this scripture multiple times in this book, but it paints a clear picture of what is going to happen at the end of days. This

Chapter 21: How to Prepare

shows us how truly separated we are from God's law that commands us to love one another. I would dare to say that raping women, tearing their babies from their womb, or smashing children on the streets is far worse than just "not loving someone." We have seen instances like this throughout history, but not to the same extent that we see it in this verse. Also, remember that the demons we have today were the predecessors to these "aliens." They will have the same nature as their ancestors.

I will conclude this book with a story that I believe will bring you hope. A couple of years ago, I was genuinely concerned and troubled about the end of days and how close I believe they are. I went to sleep and had a dream. The dream went as follows:

I was in a house with my sister, my sons, and my wife. Aliens had invaded, and they were killing one out of every three people with some kind of death ray that immediately vaporized them. I knew we had to get to safety and hide. I saw a ship pursuing us quickly, and we all jumped into a hole in the ground that looked like a basement to a house that had been obliterated. I frantically tried to figure out how to hide everyone and keep from being seen, or two people would die for sure. There was nothing I could do. I was hopeless. Then, I said to myself, "I will just let the Lord protect us. There is nothing I can do in my own power. If we are to die, then we will die and be with the Lord. Only He can save us." The alien ship flew overhead, inspected our hiding place, then left without seeing any of us. I knew that the Lord had hid us and protected us.

In conclusion, this may be a dark time that we are about to enter. However, it is a time when we can find hope and assurance in the Lord. Though the days are difficult, we can place our full trust and assurance in the Lord of heaven. When we make Him our solid foundation, nothing will shake us.

Have hope. Trust in the Lord. We will be doing amazing things in these last times, and so will our children. It will be incredible to see what we will all do. It even tells us in Daniel that we will be the only real resistance against the Antichrist that defeats him in battle. Jesus always wins. The fact that He utterly defeated the Enemy at the cross is enough for us to know that the victory over these beasts is already ours.

The Mark of the Beast

Shalom! May the Lord's face shine upon you. May you be blessed in His favor all your days. May your heart be strengthened by His love and kindness. May your eyes and heart be enlightened to the power and lovingkindness of God. Do not fear, for the Lord your God is with you always, unto the end of the age and beyond.

About the Authors

Robyn and Brandi Cunningham are the founders of Fireside Grace, which was birthed to help individuals, ministries, and cities live to their full potential through Christ-based discipleship. Using the gifts of the Spirit, they teach truth to bring clarity to the body of Christ on issues that seem confusing in this modern age. They have a YouTube channel called Fireside Grace Ministries.

The Cunningham's goal to is to guide the church body by connecting the ethics, values, character, and morals of our ancestors into the present and future generations by creatively bringing the wisdom of the past, the wisdom of the Ancient of Days, and the wisdom of our elders into the present—and bridging the gaps of the generations in between. Together, Robyn and Brandi cover topics such as current issues, dream interpretation, learning how to hear God's voice, anointing, slaying sacred cows, and much more.

Robyn and Brandi are ordained under Michael French with Patria Ministries. They have been involved with various areas of ministry for the last ten years and travel full-time, writing, speaking, and leading worship together. They minister very often to families considering abortion, helping them feel safe and supported enough to choose to parent, with a firm belief in the importance of teaching about the family unit. Brandi does professional life coaching and is a dog trainer, and believes that all dogs deserve a chance. The Cunninghams are based out of Arkansas, run an animal sanctuary, and have incredible children.

To contact the Cunninghams, visit www.FiresideGrace.com.

Subscribe to their YouTube channel: Tomorrow's Headlines, Today! https://www.youtube.com/@tomorrowsheadlinestodayfir7975

Other Books by the Authors:

The Dream Symbol Guide

Do you ever wonder what your dreams mean?

The parabolic language of dreams has long since been a mystery. Dreams invoke a thirst for supernatural understanding, and oftentimes lead many into new levels of spiritual awareness. With the plethora of dream symbols, dictionaries, and teachers, Brandi and Robyn saw a need for a Christian dream dictionary that would not only give an answer for what a symbol means, but would also give instructions about how to discern the meaning of dream symbols and equip readers to rely on the Holy Spirit to help interpret their dreams.

The Dream Symbol Guide unpacks thirteen different categories of symbols, with hundreds of entries covering many common and unique things that are in people's dreams, along with helpful teaching and perspective from Robyn and Brandi to assist you on the journey of understanding your dreams.

For more information, visit www.FiresideGrace.com.

Other Books by the Authors:

The Character of Christ

Character, in its simplest form, is the display of who we are when put under fire or to the test. This is when we see the fruit of who we are shining brightly. The Bible makes it clear that it is important for us to "bear good fruit" in season and out of season. This makes sense because it aligns with the character of Christ. He bore healthy fruit for all to see at all times and persevered through the fieriest of the trials a human could face. He showed us that we, too, possess the ability to remain the same yesterday, today, and tomorrow, despite the trials and circumstances that may arise.

Join us and the remnant as we grow and become strong enough in Jesus to press on through any amount of persecution that is here or may come!

"I am fully convinced that now, more than ever, what the Body of Christ needs more than anything else is the character of Christ."

~Brandi, Fireside Grace Ministries

For more information, visit www.FiresideGrace.com.

Other Books by the Authors:

Expel the Jezebel in Me

The spirit of Jezebel is running rampant in our country!

In this day and age, the spirit of Jezebel can be found on our TVs, in our music, in our schools, and almost everywhere you look around you. But what if I told you that the Jezebel spirit could also be influencing your actions from areas in your life where you haven't allowed Jesus to shine His light?

Expel the Jezebel in Me is a thirty-day devotional to help you see Jezebellic tendencies in yourself or others and shine light on the pathway to freedom. Each day presents a different trait of the spirit of Jezebel and how to recognize, expose, and expel it.

If you've blamed someone for being a Jezebel or have been wounded by the label of a Jezebel, this devotional is for you. It is time to get set free, learn the tools, and help others find freedom too!

For more information, visit www.FiresideGrace.com.

Other Books by the Authors:

The Pathway to Transcendent Peace

You can experience peace and joy DAILY. Right here, right now!

This book contains the information that's going to set you and so many others FREE from EVERYTHING that holds you back from TOTAL emersion in the peace of the Lord! For too long, Satan has kept us from being consistently in a place of peace that surpasses understanding.

Join me as we begin to recognize and get free from peace robbing behaviors, and developing habits that will forever keep us in that perfect place of Shalom peace.

For more information, visit www.FiresideGrace.com.

Other Books by the Authors:

Jesus Wants to Spend Time with You!

This delightful book is designed to help children understand that Jesus wants nothing more than to spend time and build a relationship with them.

Filled with twenty-four full color pages, Jesus Wants to Spend Time with You will not only entertain your child, but also serves as a tool to help get God's Word into their hearts with memory verses and truth from the Bible.

For more information, visit www.FiresideGrace.com.

Why Choose Life Coaching?

As a life coach, Brandi Cunningham's job is to motivate you and help you develop the skills that it takes to continually stay motivated, even when no ones there to motivate you.

Maybe you don't know your purpose, or your calling. But just because it's not clear to you, doesn't mean you don't have one. Everyone has one!

Maybe you know your passion and calling but are not seeing the results you want because you're only able to halfheartedly devote your life to your calling, all the while feeling social and economic pressure to make money to pay the bills.

I'm here to help you save energy and time so that you can use it more on what you're passionate about, until you can do your passion, FULL TIME!

You see, you're unique. You have been made with skills are passions I do not have, and I need you—the world needs you. I won't just stand by and watch people die inside to depression, suicide, or anger because they had no one to help show them the way.

I'm here to help show you, and help you walk in that way. You can do this! Will you let us help?

Email them at FiresideGrace@gmail.com for more information regarding availability for coaching.

www.ingramcontent.com/pod-product-compliance
Lightning Source LLC
Chambersburg PA
CBHW070058080526
44586CB00013B/1104